HOUGHTON MIFFLIN
ENGLISH

Shirley Haley-James   John Warren Stewig

Kenneth William Bierly
Jacqueline L. Chaparro
Helen Felsenthal
Norman A. Felsenthal
Michael C. Flanigan

Mary Mercer Krogness
Harry D. Laub
Nancy C. Millett
Paula J. Parris
Judy Griswold Parsons

Joy Harris Schlagal
Robert C. Schlagal
June Grant Shane
Helen J. Throckmorton

HOUGHTON MIFFLIN COMPANY · BOSTON
Atlanta · Dallas · Geneva, Illinois · Hopewell, New Jersey · Palo Alto · Toronto

Acknowledgments

Table of contents and index from *The Friendly Dolphins,* by Patricia Lauber. Random House, 1963. Reprinted by permission of Random House, Inc.

Dictionary excerpts, © 1979 Houghton Mifflin Company. Reprinted by permission from *Beginning Dictionary.*

"Pete at the Zoo," from *The World of Gwendolyn Brooks,* by Gwendolyn Brooks. Copyright © 1960 by Gwendolyn Brooks. Reprinted by permission of Harper & Row, Publishers, Inc.

"Sky Day Dream," from *Seeing Things: A Book of Poems,* by Robert Froman. Copyright © 1974 by Robert Froman. Reprinted by permission of Thomas Y. Crowell Company, and Curtis Brown Ltd.

"Summer Song," from *The Man Who Sang the Sillies,* by John Ciardi. Copyright © 1961 by John Ciardi. Reprinted by permission of J. B. Lippincott Publishers.

"Why the Sun and the Moon Live in the Sky," by Elphinstone Dayrell, from *Why the Sun and the Moon Live in the Sky,* by Blair Lent (Houghton Mifflin Company, 1968).

Printed in U.S.A.

ISBN: 0-395-31910-2

Contents

4

The Sentence

1 | What Is a Sentence?

When you were very little, you spoke only one or two words. You may have pointed to a toy and said, "Toy."

The word *toy* names something, but it does not tell a complete thought. It does not tell who owns the toy. It does not tell what happened to the toy.

As you grew older, you learned to speak in sentences. A **sentence** is a group of words that tells a complete thought. When you use sentences, people understand what you want to say. Look at the sentences below.

> This is my toy. My toy is broken.

These sentences tell who owns the toy and what happened to it. Each sentence tells a complete thought. Notice that each sentence begins with a capital letter and ends with a period.

Try It Out

Read each group of words aloud. Tell which groups of words are sentences.

1. Ate cheese.
2. Alice laughed loudly.
3. Walked quickly.
4. He talked softly.
5. I'm lost.
6. The gray kitten.
7. Drank the milk.
8. We are friends.

> ▸ A **sentence** is a group of words that tells a complete thought.

Written Practice

A. Read each group of words below. If the group of words is a sentence, write *sentence*. If the group of words is not a sentence, write *not a sentence*.

1. Polly went to the movies.
2. The cat chased the chipmunk.
3. Began to sink.
4. The teacher read to the children.
5. Landed on the runway.
6. The bird.
7. The leaves turned yellow and red.
8. Alice wrote.
9. The rocky mountain.
10. The dog buried its bone.
11. Did not like the story.

B. Read each group of words. Write the groups of words that are sentences.

12. Like to swim.
    We like to swim.
13. Miguel came home.
    Came home late.
14. To the show.
    Ben went to the show.
15. Jill plays well.
    Plays well.
16. The melted snow.
    He loves the snow.
17. Is raining.
    It is raining hard.
18. Maria plays soccer.
    Plays soccer well.
19. Leroy will join us.
    Will not join.
20. The football team.
    The team lost.
21. We went to school.
    To school each day.

- **Writing Sentences** Write five sentences about something you like to do. Be sure to make each sentence a complete thought.

2 | Word Order

Sometimes you can change the order of the words in a sentence and still have the sentence make sense. The sentences below have the same words, but the word order is different. Read each sentence. Notice that each sentence makes sense but has a different meaning.

The cat chased the dog.   The dog chased the cat.

Try It Out

Read each sentence aloud. Make another sentence by changing the word order.

1. The ducklings followed the mother duck.
2. The children quietly watch the ducks.
3. The ducks move closer to see the children.

Changing the order of the words can change the meaning of a sentence.

Written Practice

Read each sentence below. Write another sentence by changing the word order.

1. Lori asks Paul about the hike.
2. Paul gives Lori the map.
3. Paul shows Lori the trail.
4. The trail is wider than the pond.
5. Lori sees a mountain goat.

3 | Statements and Questions

There are different kinds of sentences. One kind of sentence *tells* you something. A sentence that tells something is called a **statement**. A statement always starts with a capital letter and ends with a period. The sentences below are statements.

Kirk is a good runner.
He jogs every day.

Another kind of sentence *asks* you something. A sentence that asks something is called a **question**. A question starts with a capital letter and ends with a question mark. The sentences below are questions.

Have you ever seen Claudia run?
How fast can she run?

Try It Out

Read each sentence. Tell if the sentence is a question or a statement. Tell what mark should come at the end of each sentence.

1. Peg is nine years old
2. Is Peg in the third grade
3. What is Peg's favorite sport
4. I hope it is softball
5. She can play on my team

> ▶ A sentence that tells something is called a **statement**. A statement begins with a capital letter and ends with a period.
>
> ▶ A sentence that asks something is called a **question**. A question begins with a capital letter and ends with a question mark.

Written Practice

A. Read each sentence below. If it is a statement, write *statement*. If it is a question, write *question*.

1. My friend's name is Carlos.
2. Where is Carlos?
3. Carlos and I like to play soccer.
4. Would you like to play?
5. We are having a game on Friday.
6. Let's find Carlos.

B. Write each sentence. Start with a capital letter. End with the correct mark.

7. do you like to visit the zoo
8. what is your favorite animal
9. the monkey is my favorite animal
10. have you seen the monkeys climb trees
11. they never fall, even when they jump
12. they use their tails to help them balance
13. do you like to watch the baby monkeys

- **Writing Sentences** Write two statements about the zoo. Write three questions about zoo animals. Begin and end your sentences correctly.

4 | Exclamations

If you saw a baseball player hit a home run, you might shout, "It's a home run!" When you talk about something exciting, your voice changes. You *sound* excited.

A sentence that shows strong feeling is called an **exclamation**. An exclamation can show excitement, anger, surprise, or fear. An exclamation ends with a special mark. It is called an **exclamation mark** (!).

Try It Out

A. Read these sentences aloud. Make your voice show strong feeling.

Gina, look! The ball is rolling down the street! Here comes a car! Be careful!

B. Read these sentences aloud. Then change each statement to an exclamation. Read the exclamations aloud with strong feeling.

Here's the cave. I can't wait to go in it. Be careful, Jim. I just fell. Let's get out of here.

> ▶ An **exclamation** is a sentence that shows strong feeling. Use an **exclamation mark** (!) at the end of an exclamation.

Written Practice

A. Write these sentences, using capital letters and the correct end mark.

1. next week is my birthday
2. i can hardly wait
3. mom said I could have a party
4. would you like to come
5. the party will be on Saturday
6. we will have a picnic outside
7. do you like hamburgers
8. i'm getting a puppy for my birthday
9. a puppy is just what I wanted
10. will Saturday ever come

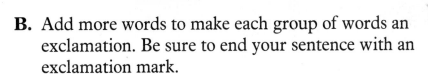

B. Add more words to make each group of words an exclamation. Be sure to end your sentence with an exclamation mark.

Example: your prize   Your prize costs so much!

11. the fire
12. a parade
13. a birthday party
14. the big storm
15. the race
16. a lost kitten
17. a good report card
18. my trip
19. a fight
20. my new bike

- **Writing Sentences** Write five sentences about your birthday. Make at least one of your sentences an exclamation.

5 | The Subject of the Sentence

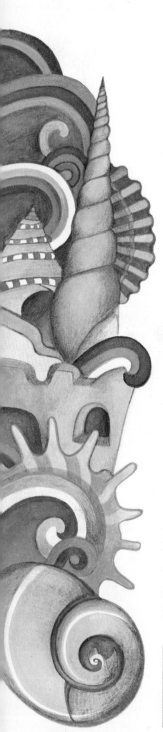

Every sentence has two parts. One part of the sentence is called the subject. The **subject** tells who or what the sentence is about.

In each sentence below, the subject is underlined. The subject can be one word or more than one word. Read each sentence. Who or what is the sentence about?

<u>Sammy</u> likes to see movies.
<u>Sammy's sister</u> goes to the movies.
<u>The old movie house</u> is down the street.
<u>Sammy and his sister</u> walked there together.

You can always find the subject of a sentence by asking, Who or what is the sentence about?

Try It Out

Read each sentence aloud. Tell the subject of each sentence.

1. The children made a sand castle at the beach.
2. The sand was wet.
3. Beautiful shells lay on the sand.
4. The sandy beach was crowded with people.
5. The sky and the water were so blue!
6. The strong waves splashed on the beach.

> ▶ The **subject** is the part of a sentence that tells who or what the sentence is about.

Written Practice

A. Read each sentence. Then write the subject of the sentence. Remember, the subject tells who or what the sentence is about.

1. Joey liked to fish.
2. Tina liked to fish, too.
3. The lake was the best place for fishing.
4. Their fishing poles were new.
5. Earthworms were the best bait.
6. Bullfrogs jumped out of the water.
7. Joey and Tina caught two bass.
8. One fish got away.
9. The children's parents cooked the fish.
10. The fish dinner was delicious.

B. Write a sentence by adding a subject to each group of words.

11. _____ had a softball game.
12. _____ was fun.
13. _____ were the two captains of the teams.
14. _____ were on each team.
15. _____ was the pitcher.
16. _____ hit a home run.
17. _____ caught a fly ball.
18. _____ shouted and cheered.
19. _____ had won the game.
20. _____ had a wonderful time.

6 | The Predicate of the Sentence

You know that a sentence has two parts. The subject tells who or what the sentence is about. The other part of the sentence is called the predicate. The **predicate** tells what the subject does or is.

The sentences below are divided between the subject and the predicate.

> Jason / plays the flute.
> His cousin / is a good singer.

What are the subjects of the sentences? *Jason* and *His cousin* are the subjects.

Look at the first sentence again. If *Jason* is the subject, what is the predicate? Which words tell what *Jason* does or is? The predicate is *plays the flute*.

Now look at the second sentence. Since *His cousin* is the subject, what is the predicate? Which words tell what *His cousin* does or is? *Is a good singer* is the predicate.

Try It Out

Read these sentences aloud. Tell the subject and predicate of each sentence.

1. The merry-go-round is a favorite ride.
2. The roller coaster climbs the steep hill.
3. Music floats through the park.
4. A man and a monkey sell balloons.
5. The sun shines brightly.
6. We bought a ticket for a ride.

Every sentence has two parts.
▶ The **subject** tells who or what the sentence is about.
▶ The **predicate** tells what the subject does or is.

Written Practice

A. Write each sentence. Circle the predicate.

1. Emily takes swimming lessons.
2. Sam learns how to swim, too.
3. Emily and Sam go to the lessons together.
4. Their lesson is one hour long.
5. The two children listen carefully.
6. The coach teaches Emily and Sam the crawl.
7. A lifeguard watches the swimmers.
8. Everyone follows the safety rules.

B. Write these sentences. Draw a line between the subject and predicate. The first one is done for you.

9. The forest animals listened for danger.
   The forest animals / listened for danger.
10. The snowshoe rabbit perked up its ears.
11. The white-tailed deer leaped over the logs.
12. A blue jay and a robin flew away.
13. A gray squirrel chattered in its nest.
14. Each animal ran to its home.

C. Write a sentence. Add a predicate to each subject.

15. The gray pony ____.
16. A sled ____.
17. A tall girl ____.
18. The baby ____.
19. The rose ____.
20. A snowstorm ____.

The Predicate of the Sentence   **19**

7 | Separating Sentences

Read the story below.

> Tanya likes to water-ski have you ever tried to water-ski look at how fast she goes across the water.

Was the story hard to read? Why? Without end marks and capital letters, the sentences run together. You do not know where one sentence ends and another sentence begins.

You know that a sentence ends with a period, a question mark, or an exclamation mark. The mark at the end of a sentence tells you where to stop and take a breath.

Now read the story again. Let the end marks and capital letters help you read the sentences.

> Tanya likes to water-ski. Have you ever tried to water-ski? Look at how fast she goes across the water!

Try It Out

Read this story aloud. Tell where you would separate the sentences with capital letters and end marks.

> Pedro likes to paint he spends many hours practicing would you like to see his pictures?

Do not run your sentences together. Use a capital letter to begin each sentence. End each sentence with the correct mark.

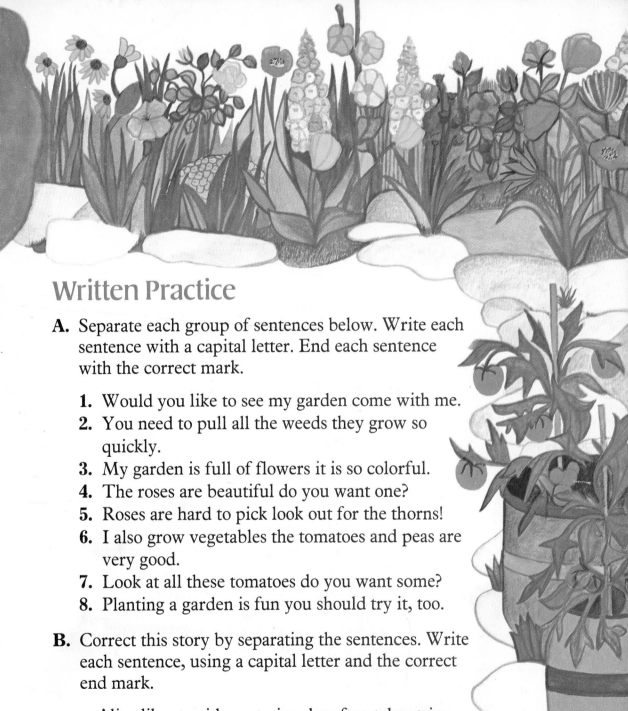

Written Practice

A. Separate each group of sentences below. Write each sentence with a capital letter. End each sentence with the correct mark.

1. Would you like to see my garden come with me.
2. You need to pull all the weeds they grow so quickly.
3. My garden is full of flowers it is so colorful.
4. The roses are beautiful do you want one?
5. Roses are hard to pick look out for the thorns!
6. I also grow vegetables the tomatoes and peas are very good.
7. Look at all these tomatoes do you want some?
8. Planting a garden is fun you should try it, too.

B. Correct this story by separating the sentences. Write each sentence, using a capital letter and the correct end mark.

    Alice likes to ride on trains she often takes trips on them the train travels through cities does it go through the country, too the train moves quickly there are many things to see along the way.

8 | Using Words Correctly

gone, went

Look at the underlined words in these sentences.

I <u>went</u> swimming.   I have <u>gone</u> swimming.
He <u>went</u> skating.   He <u>has gone</u> skating.

The sentences on the left show that *went* needs no helping word. Use *have* or *has* with *gone*.

> Use the helping word *has* or *have* with *gone*. *Went* does not need a helping word.

Practice

A. Choose the correct word to complete each sentence.

My class (gone, went) to the circus. We have (gone, went) before. José has (gone, went) to watch the clowns. Polly (gone, went) to watch the acrobats.

B. Write the word that completes each sentence.

1. Karen (gone, went) to the store.
2. She has (went, gone) with her friend Bruce.
3. Jake (went, gone) to the swimming pool.
4. Lisa and Fred have (went, gone) with Jake.

- **Writing Sentences** Write three sentences using *gone* correctly and two using *went*.

saw, seen

Look at the underlined words in these sentences.

I saw a hawk.   I have seen a hawk.
He saw an eagle.   He has seen an eagle.

The sentences on the left show that *saw* needs no helping word. The ones on the right use *have* or *has* with *seen*.

> Use the helping word *has* or *have* with *seen*. *Saw* does not need a helping word.

Practice

A. Choose the correct word to complete each sentence.

I (saw, seen) a chipmunk sitting on a rock. It was the first time I have (saw, seen) one sitting so still. I asked Bobby if he (saw, seen) it. He said he has (saw, seen) so many chipmunks before that he hardly noticed it.

B. Write the word that completes each sentence.

1. I (saw, seen) geese flying south for the winter.
2. Sara has (saw, seen) squirrels looking for nuts.
3. My father has (saw, seen) red foxes in their den.
4. Once Larry and I (saw, seen) beavers swimming.
5. Carolyn said she (saw, seen) a bat in a cave.
6. My brothers have (saw, seen) baby robins.

- **Writing Sentences** Write two sentences, using *saw* correctly. Write three more sentences, using *seen* correctly.

9 Building Vocabulary

Using Word Clues

How do you find the meaning of a new word? You can use the dictionary. You can also use clues in sentences. Often, other words in the sentence will give a clue to the meaning of the word you do not know. Sometimes another sentence will explain the meaning of a word.

Read the sentences below. Using the clues in the sentences, decide what the underlined word means.

Two colorful <u>teals</u> swam in the peaceful lake. They quacked softly as they swam along.

What are teals?

a. fish   **b.** people   **c.** ducks

The clues in the sentences tell you that teals swim and quack. What swim and quack?

Practice

A. Read each group of sentences. Then answer the question that follows it by choosing *a*, *b*, or *c*. Use the clues in the sentences to help you.

   1. The <u>courageous</u> hunter explored the jungle. He was not afraid of the danger.
   What does <u>courageous</u> mean?
   a. scared   **b.** brave   **c.** funny

2. Linda is <u>intelligent</u>. She learns very quickly.
   What does <u>intelligent</u> mean?
   a. smart   **b**. lazy   **c**.friendly

3. Victor was a <u>rude</u> child. He talked back to his
   parents and even to his teacher.
   What does <u>rude</u> mean?
   a. polite   **b**. having bad manners   **c**. nice

4. Richard got <u>drenched</u> on the way home.
   Everything he had on was soaked by the rain.
   What does <u>drenched</u> mean?
   a. very wet   **b**. dry   **c**. tired

5. The <u>toucan</u> flew to the branch of the tree. It
   had a large bill and beautiful feathers.
   What is a <u>toucan</u>?
   a. an insect   **b**. a plane   **c**. a bird

B. Read each group of sentences. Write the meaning of
the underlined word by using clues in the sentences.
The first one is done for you.

6. <u>Cashews</u> are my favorite nuts. I like their
   curved shape.
   Cashews are nuts that have a curved shape.

7. We saw an African movie about an <u>impala</u>. I
   was amazed that it had such long legs and
   curved horns.

8. I found little <u>aphids</u> sticking to my plant. I
   brushed them off, but those insects flew back to
   eat my plant.

9. The <u>cantaloupe</u> we ate was sweet and juicy. It is
   my favorite kind of melon.

10. The woman held her silk <u>parasol</u> over her head.
    She used the small umbrella to keep the sun out
    of her eyes.

Review

- **What Is a Sentence?** *(pp. 9–10)*   Write the group of words that makes a complete sentence.

    1. Look at the clouds.   **3.** Heard thunder.
    The dark clouds.   I heard thunder.
    2. The sun has gone.   **4.** Starting to rain.
    The sun away.   It's starting to rain.

- **Word Order** *(p. 11)*   Write another sentence by changing the order of the words.

    5. Did Paula see Monica on the playground?
    6. After the girls played on the swings, they played on the jungle gym.
    7. Playing basketball is more fun than playing tag.
    8. Did the girls see the teacher wave?
    9. The children followed the teacher into the room.

- **Statements and Questions** *(pp. 12–13)*   Look at the sentences you wrote for the exercise above. For each statement, write *S*. For each question, write *Q*.

- **Exclamations** *(pp. 14–15)*   Write each sentence. Use the correct end mark.

    10. It is such a beautiful day
    11. Tony and Jane walk to the beach
    12. Will they go swimming
    13. They race into the water
    14. How cold the water is

- **The Subject of the Sentence** *(pp. 16–17)* Read the sentences. Write the subject of each sentence.

  15. The children tiptoed into the library.
  16. The library's new books lay on the shelf.
  17. The book shelves filled the room.
  18. The teacher read a story.

- **The Predicate of the Sentence** *(pp. 18–19)* Write the predicate of each sentence in the exercise above.

- **Separating Sentences** *(pp. 20–21)* Rewrite the story below by separating the sentences.

    Our family planned a vacation we wanted to camp in the mountains. First we went shopping for food then we rolled up our sleeping bags we put them in the car off we went.

- **Using Words Correctly** *(pp. 22–23)* Write the word that correctly completes each sentence.

  19. We (gone, went) to the flower show.
  20. Nick has (gone, went) to see the show too.
  21. We (saw, seen) tiny Japanese trees at the show.
  22. May and Sam already have (saw, seen) the roses.

- **Building Vocabulary** *(pp. 24–25)* Write the meaning of the underlined word by using word clues.

  23. The lion has a ferocious roar.
      a. quiet   **b.** fierce
  24. Grant was concerned about his sick dog.
      a. happy   **b.** worried
  25. The awkward puppy kept tripping and falling.
      a. clumsy   **b.** brown

Listening and Speaking

1 | What Is Listening?

The world is full of sounds. You hear them, and you know what they are. Most of the time, you do not really listen to them.

Pat's mother asked her, "Isn't the water boiling yet?"

"Well, I hear it now," she answered. "But I wasn't listening for it before."

Everyone has experiences like that. You hear a sound, but you do not really notice it. Listening and hearing are different. When you listen, you pay careful attention to what you are hearing.

Usually you have a reason for listening. Someone gets your attention. Your teacher says, "Okay, everyone. It's time to listen. I am going to read a story now." You know it is time to pay attention and listen. A new friend says, "This is how you get to my house." You need the directions, so you listen.

Sometimes a sound gets your attention. You hear a siren outside your school. You listen to hear if the siren is stopping near your school. You hear the doorbell ring while you are busy cleaning your room. You listen to hear who is there.

What other reasons can you think of for listening?

Practice

A. Try to remember what sounds you heard in the last five minutes. Write them down. Are the sounds you wrote down sounds you often hear?

B. Now listen carefully for several minutes. Write down the sounds you heard. Are there some new sounds that you did not hear earlier?

2 | Being a Good Listener

Listening takes work. You must pay attention to what someone says or to sounds you hear. Follow these hints to become a better listener.

1. Decide that you are going to listen. Then block out other sounds or other people talking. Do not try to listen to more than one thing at a time.
2. Do not daydream or let your mind wander. Look at the person who is talking, not out the window. If your mind does wander, look at the person who is talking. Pay attention again.
3. Be polite when you listen. Do not interrupt the person who is speaking. Let the person know that you are listening. You can nod your head or smile to show that you understand something. If you look confused, the speaker will know that something needs to be explained.
4. Pay attention to how people talk. How people say things helps you know what they mean. Someone who is excited may speak loudly or quickly. Someone who is sad may speak quietly. People's voices go up and down. When asking a question, what sometimes happens to the person's voice?

Practice

Listen as your teacher reads some sentences to you. Be ready to tell whether your teacher sounds angry, sad, excited, or curious.

3 | Listening for Main Ideas and Details

Main Ideas

The **main idea** of a story is what the story is about. After you read a story, you can tell what the main idea of the story is.

When someone talks, you can listen for a main idea. Think about what the person is talking about. What is the person telling you?

Jane and Harriet were talking. Read what they said.

> Harriet asked Jane, "Have you ever heard of a koala?"
>
> "No, what is it?" answered Jane.
>
> Harriet told her, "It's an animal that looks like a bear. It isn't a bear, though. It has large ears, small, bright eyes, and no tail. It's not very big, and it lives in trees in Australia."

What is the main idea of what Harriet told Jane? The main idea is *what is a koala.*

Practice

Listen carefully as your teacher reads. Be ready to tell the main idea of the paragraph.

Details

Listening for details is also important. **Details** are facts and other information that tell about the main idea.

Tommy's mother left him an important message. Read the message.

> Tommy, I will be late coming home from work today. I want you to go to Scott's house after school. Scott's mother knows that you are coming. I'll pick you up at 5:30.   Mom

The main idea of this message is that Tommy's mother will be late. There are three details for Tommy to remember. The first is to go to Scott's house. Another is that Scott's mother knows that he is coming. The last is that Tommy's mother will pick him up at 5:30.

What other times would listening for details be important?

Practice

Listen as your teacher reads to you. Be ready to tell the main idea and the details that tell about the main idea.

4 | How to Be a Good Speaker

Walter and Doris both brought their pets to school for show and tell. Which student was the better speaker?

WALTER: This is my pet rabbit, Happy. I've had him since he was a tiny baby. Now he weighs six pounds. He eats lettuce and special food. He's a good pet.

DORIS: Um, this is my guinea pig. Um, well, I like having a guinea pig for a pet. He, ah, does lots of neat things. He, um, that's all.

Walter's report was easier to listen to. He knew what he wanted to say. He said it smoothly.

Doris seemed less sure of what to say. She filled her report with words like *ah* and *um*.

Speaking well, like reading, writing, and listening, is a skill. It takes practice. Follow these hints to be a better speaker.

1. Speak clearly. Pronounce all your words.
2. Do not talk too loudly or too softly.
3. Look at the people you are talking to.
4. Wait your turn to speak. It is not polite to talk when someone else is talking.
5. Think about what you want to say. Do not use *ah*'s, *well*'s, and *um*'s when you speak.

Practice

Get together with a classmate. Think of a short talk you can give on one of these subjects.

a game I like
my favorite time of day
a movie or television show I like

Give a short talk on one of the subjects above. Take turns being the speaker and the listener. Tell your classmate how well he or she spoke. Use these questions as a guide.

1. Did the speaker speak clearly?
2. Did the speaker talk too loudly or softly?
3. Did the speaker look at the listener?
4. Did the speaker use many *ah*'s, *well*'s, and *um*'s?

5 | Introducing People

Leroy just moved next door to Jeff. Leroy and Jeff have met and are outside playing together. When Peter went by, Jeff called him over. Read how Jeff introduced Peter and Leroy.

Jeff said, "Peter, this is our new neighbor, Leroy. He just moved here from Idaho. He's going to be in our class."

Then Jeff turned to Leroy and said, "Leroy, this is Peter. Peter and I have been friends for a long time. We're in Scouts together."

When you introduce people, say their names and something about them. When Peter came by, Jeff introduced him to Leroy. Jeff helped Peter and Leroy start talking by telling something about each boy. What did he tell about Leroy and Peter?

Follow these hints when you introduce people.

1. Look at the people you are introducing.
2. Say each person's name you are introducing.
3. Tell something about the people you are introducing.
4. Speak clearly.

Practice

Get together with two other classmates. Pretend that your classmates do not know each other. Introduce each of them. Remember to tell something about each person to help them start talking. Take turns making the introductions.

6 | Having Conversations

People get to know one another by talking. You meet a student on a school bus or in a playground. You start talking to each other. You find out you both have a dog or you both like to sing.

Friends get to know each other better by talking. You tell friends about things you have done. You ask how a friend feels about something.

You talk to your family. You tell your mother about something funny that happened. Your uncle tells you something he did when he was your age.

All of these kinds of talks are called conversations. **Conversations** are friendly talks that people have. They can be about many different ideas.

Read this conversation among three friends.

KATHY: When is the trip to the TV station?

DAN: I think it's on Thursday.

JILL: Yes, it's on Thursday. I'm really excited! Do you think we'll be on TV?

DAN: They'll probably just show us around. That's what happened when I went to the radio station.

KATHY: I didn't know you had done that. Was it fun?

DAN: Oh, yes. I saw a disc jockey play records and give a weather report. The weather report was funny because he laughed when he read it.

JILL: Maybe we'll see the TV weather reporter on our trip. Do you remember when he came to school?

KATHY: I do. He showed us a film about weather. I didn't know there were different kinds of clouds.

JILL: I didn't either. I hope our TV trip will be fun.

DAN: I bet it will be better than the radio trip.

In this conversation, everyone took turns talking. Kathy, Dan, and Jill listened to each other. They did not interrupt each other. They talked about many things.

A conversation often starts with a question. How did this one start? Who answered Kathy's question?

After Dan told about the radio station, what did Kathy say? She found out something about Dan that she had not known.

Then Jill spoke and asked a question. Questions can keep a conversation going. What did you find out because Jill asked her question? New information or ideas also keep a conversation going. Who added new ideas or information?

Follow these hints to have good conversations.
1. Do not interrupt. Let each person speak.
2. Listen to each person.
3. Ask questions if you have them.
4. Add new ideas if you have them.
5. Be friendly.

Practice

Get together with two or more classmates. Have a conversation together. You might want to start by talking about something you have recently done at home or at school. Use these questions as a guide.

1. Do I try not to interrupt? Do I let each person talk?
2. Do I listen to each person?
3. Do I ask questions if I have them?
4. Do I add information or new ideas if I have them?
5. Am I friendly?

7 | Using the Telephone

Do you sometimes talk to a friend on the telephone? It is important to be polite when you talk on the phone. Susan called her friend Lois. Here is the conversation they had.

LOIS: Hello.

SUSAN: Hi, Lois. This is Susan.

LOIS: Hi, Susan.

SUSAN: Do you want to go to the library with me after school tomorrow? Maybe we can play together for a while, too.

LOIS: That would be fun. Let me ask my mother. Hold on. (Lois goes to ask her mother.) Hi. She said I could go.

SUSAN: Good. I'll see you tomorrow at school. Okay?

LOIS: Okay, bye.

SUSAN: Goodbye.

Notice that Susan and Lois said *hello* and *hi* at the beginning of their talk. Susan said her name so that Lois would know who was calling. Then she told why she was calling. Why did Lois tell Susan to hold on? At the end of their phone call, the girls said goodbye to each other.

Sometimes a phone call is for someone else. If that person is not home, you may have to take a message for him or her. On the next page read what Seth said when the phone rang.

SETH: Hello.

MR. LERNER: Hello. This is Mr. Lerner. May I please speak to your dad?

SETH: I'm sorry, Mr. Lerner. He's not here. This is Seth. May I take a message for him?

MR. LERNER: Yes, Seth. Please tell him that I'll bring him the tools he wants on Saturday morning at nine.

SETH: Okay, Mr. Lerner. At nine o'clock Saturday morning, you'll bring over the tools.

MR. LERNER: Right. Thanks, Seth. Goodbye.

SETH: You're welcome. Goodbye.

Notice that Seth asked if he could take a message for his father. He repeated the message to be sure he understood it. Seth wrote the message down, so he would not forget it. Here is the message he wrote.

Dad, Mr. Lerner called. He'll bring over the tools Saturday morning at 9:00. Seth.

Seth wrote *Dad* on the message. Then he wrote the message and signed his name. Why do you think he wrote *Dad* on the note? Why did he sign his name?

Practice

Get together with a classmate. Practice having these telephone conversations.

1. Ask a classmate what time the school play starts on Thursday night.

2. Take a message for your mother. Your Aunt Carla called and said, "I will stop by on Thursday at 5:30. If that's not all right, have her call me."

3. Ask a friend to a picnic at your house. Tell when the picnic will be and what to bring.

8 | Giving a Talk

Have you ever given a report to your class? When you talk before a group of people, you should talk about a topic you know well. You must know what you want to say before you say it. You should plan the order in which you will tell things. You may want to write some notes to help yourself remember what you will say. Notes should not be complete sentences. You are not going to read your talk.

Speak clearly so that your listeners can understand what you are saying. Remember to talk loudly enough. Do not talk too fast or too slowly. Sound interested in what you are saying, and your listeners will be interested, too.

Remember to look at the group. Do not look down or around. If the group looks puzzled, you can explain a little more.

This is how Julia got ready to tell about a time she ate in a Chinese restaurant.

She thought the first thing she would tell is where the restaurant is and why she went there. Then she would tell what she ate. Next, she would tell what she liked best about her experience. She wrote down some notes to help her remember what she wanted to talk about.

Ideas for Talk

1. where I went
2. why I went
3. what I ate
4. what I liked best

Julia did not write down every word she would say. Her notes just reminded her of what she wanted to talk about. When Julia gave her talk, she looked at her notes two or three times. Here is the talk Julia gave.

We went to the Shanghai Restaurant Saturday night. It's on Park Street next to the bowling alley. We went there because it was my dad's birthday. My mom and brother and I took him there as a surprise.

I had wonton soup and egg rolls. Then I had something called Moo Shi pork. Moo Shi is pork and vegetables that you roll up in some kind of pancake. It was delicious.

The best thing about the meal was eating with chopsticks. At first, I couldn't use them correctly. It became easier after our waiter showed us how to hold them. Our waiter even gave us some chopsticks to take home.

Practice

Form groups of three or four students. Choose an experience you would like to share. It might be about something that you did or saw recently. Give your talk to your group.

When you give your talk, (1) plan what you want to say, (2) make notes, (3) speak clearly, and (4) look at the group.

When you listen to someone's talk or story, (1) tell what you liked about it, and (2) tell if there was something the person could do to make it better.

Nouns

1 | What Are Nouns?

What would you like to be when you grow up? Did you name a person who does a special job like a teacher, a scientist, or a pilot?

Where do you like to go in the summer? Did you name a place like a beach, the mountains, or a park?

What are your favorite toys?

Did you name things like games, balls, or dolls?

Each of your answers to the questions named a person, place, or thing. A word that names a person, place, or thing is called a **noun**.

Try It Out

A. Look at the picture on page 42. Name all the people and things you see. Are all the people and things you named nouns?

B. Read these sentences aloud. Find all of the nouns.

1. The circus will be coming soon.
2. My sister and my brother are so excited.
3. The tent is gigantic.
4. The clowns are always funny.
5. Their hats are silly, and their shoes are floppy.
6. The elephants walk around the ring.
7. Their long trunks spray water.
8. The lions are scary.
9. Their trainer cracks the whip.
10. The ringmaster wears a large hat.
11. Many acrobats use a net.
12. The people always clap.

> ▸ A **noun** names a person, place, or thing.

Written Practice

A. Write a noun to finish each sentence below.

1. My favorite place to play is the ____.
2. My favorite game is ____.
3. I enjoy talking with my ____.
4. ____ and ____ are interesting wild animals.
5. My favorite kind of pet is a ____.
6. I would like to meet ____.
7. I like to ride on a ____.
8. If I had a garden, I would plant ____ and ____.
9. If I went to a museum, I would look at ____.
10. I enjoy eating ____ and ____.

B. Write all the nouns in each sentence.

11. The busy city was crowded.
12. The train raced along the track.
13. People lined up to buy tickets for the show.
14. Skyscrapers seemed to reach the sky.
15. The dogs chased the ducks in the park.
16. Some children fed the squirrels.
17. A man played a guitar.
18. A woman read a newspaper.
19. Cars stopped at the corner.

- **Writing Sentences** Pretend you are walking through a park. Write five sentences about it. Have each sentence tell about a person, a place, or a thing. Underline the nouns in your sentences.

2 | Singular and Plural Nouns

Read these sentences.

She tried on a <u>hat</u>.   She tried on many <u>hats</u>.

Which underlined noun names one thing? Which underlined noun names more than one thing? A noun that names only one person, place, or thing is called a **singular noun**. A noun that names more than one person, place, or thing is called a **plural noun**.

Read the sentences again. Which noun is singular? Which noun is plural?

The plural form of a noun is usually different from the singular. To write the plural of most nouns, you add -*s* to the singular form (*hat, hats*). Read the nouns below.

SINGULAR: room   friend   park
PLURAL: rooms   friends   parks

Not every noun forms the plural by adding -*s*. Singular nouns that end in -*s, -sh, -ch,* or -*x* form their plurals by adding -*es*. Look at the nouns below.

SINGULAR: class   brush   lunch   box
PLURAL: classes   brushes   lunches   boxes

Try It Out

Read each sentence aloud. Tell if the underlined nouns are singular or plural.

1. The <u>foxes</u> slept in their <u>dens</u>.
2. The <u>flags</u> fluttered in the <u>wind</u>.
3. The <u>boxes</u> were piled on the <u>porch</u>.

> ▸ **Singular nouns** name one person, place, or thing.
> ▸ **Plural nouns** name more than one person, place, or thing.
> Most singular nouns are made plural by adding -*s*.
> Singular nouns ending with -*s*, -*ch*, -*sh*, or -*x* are made plural by adding -*es*.

Written Practice

Read each sentence. Then write each underlined noun. Write *S* after the word if the noun is singular. Write *P* if the noun is plural.

1. Three dinners are listed on the board.
2. My father bought six peaches at the stand.
3. The buses waited behind the cars.
4. The bushes were blooming with flowers.
5. The tailor made five dresses.

- **Writing Sentences** Change each singular noun to plural by adding -*s* or -*es*. Then write six sentences. Use one plural noun in each sentence.

6. dish	**8.** match	**10.** tribe
7. fox	**9.** circus	**11.** glass

3 | More Plural Nouns

Most singular nouns can be changed to their plural forms by adding *-s* or *-es*. Some nouns that end with *-y* form their plurals in a different way. Look at these nouns that end in *-y*.

penny   cherry
pennies   cherries

What happened to the *-y*? What two letters are added to make each noun plural? Nouns that end in *-y* are made plural by changing the *y* to *i*, then adding *-es*.

Try It Out

Change each singular noun to its plural form.

1. baby   **2.** hobby   **3.** strawberry   **4.** family   **5.** party

> Singular nouns that end with *-y* are made plural by changing the *y* to *i*, then adding *-es*.

Written Practice

Write the plural form of each underlined noun.

1. The boys had a <u>party</u>.
2. They rode a <u>pony</u>.
3. The <u>family</u> watched.
4. The <u>puppy</u> went too.
5. They read a <u>story</u>.
6. It was about a <u>baby</u>.

- **Writing Sentences**   Write a sentence for each plural noun you wrote in the exercise above.

4 | Special Plural Nouns

Some singular nouns are made plural in a special way. Look at this noun.

Singular	**Plural**
goose	geese

What happens to the spelling of the singular noun *goose* when it becomes plural? Some singular nouns are made plural by changing the spelling of the singular noun.

Here are some other singular nouns and their special plural forms. How is each singular noun changed to the plural form?

Singular	**Plural**
man	men
woman	women
child	children
mouse	mice
tooth	teeth
foot	feet

Try It Out

Look at the word in ( ) after each sentence. Use the correct plural of that word to complete the sentence.

1. The dentist looked at all of Max's _____. (tooth)
2. The _____ tuck their heads under their wings. (goose)

3. Three _____ ran away from the black cat. (mouse)
4. Ben hopped on both _____. (foot)
5. There are many _____ on the school bus. (child)

> Some nouns are made plural by changing the
>   spelling in a special way.

Written Practice

A. Write the noun that completes each sentence.

1. Three (child, children) are reading.
2. One (woman, women) was swimming in the pool.
3. The field was full of (mouse, mice).
4. An alligator had a broken (tooth, teeth).
5. There was only one (man, men) on the beach.
6. The flock of (goose, geese) flew south.
7. It's important to brush all your (tooth, teeth).
8. Each (child, children) had a part in the play.
9. Several (man, men) visited our school.
10. We invited those (woman, women) to the meeting.

B. Write the plural form of each singular noun below.

11. child	**13.** box	**15.** mouse	**17.** woman
12. tooth	**14.** cherry	**16.** peach	**18.** dress

- **Writing Sentences** Choose five of your plural nouns from exercise B. Write a sentence for each one. Remember to begin each sentence with a capital letter and end it with the correct mark.

5 | Common and Proper Nouns

You have learned that a noun names a person, place, or thing. Some nouns name particular people, places, or things. Read the sentences below. The nouns in each sentence are underlined.

A girl waves to her friend.
Suzanna waves to Tony.

The nouns in the first sentence name any girl and any friend. A noun that names any person, place, or thing is called a **common noun**.

The nouns in the second sentence are *Suzanna* and *Tony*. *Suzanna* is the name of a particular girl. *Tony* is the name of a particular friend. A noun that names a particular person, place, or thing is called a **proper noun**.

All proper nouns begin with capital letters. The capital letters tell you that a particular person, place, or thing is being named.

A proper noun often has more than one word. Each important word in a proper noun begins with a capital letter.

Jimmy White Cloud   New York City   Lake Erie

Try It Out

Read each pair of nouns. Then decide which one is a common noun and which one is a proper noun.

Ash Road   country   Mrs. Wu   holiday
street   India   principal   Thanksgiving

> ▸ A **common noun** names any person, place, or thing.
>
> ▸ A **proper noun** names a particular person, place, or thing. Proper nouns begin with capital letters.

Written Practice

A. Make two lists on your paper. Write all the common nouns in one list. Write all the proper nouns in the other. Remember to use capital letters correctly when you write proper nouns.

planet	avenue	writer
jupiter	village	mr. ross
ocean	iowa city	friend
texas	ohio river	jeanette

B. Read each sentence below. Write the common nouns and the proper nouns. Write *C* after each common noun. Write *P* after each proper noun.

1. My family visited the Stoneham Zoo.
2. The zoo is on River Road.
3. Aaron, Jessie, and my brother came, too.
4. Patsy, a camel, munched on hay.
5. Mr. Zuchias fed the seals.
6. The fish were at the Aquarium House.
7. The sun began to set behind the trees.
8. We hated to leave Arthur the elephant.

● **Writing Sentences** Write five sentences about this picture. Use common and proper nouns in your sentences.

6 | Nouns That Show Ownership

Read the sentence below.

Sally's bike is red.

Who owns the bike? The sentence tells you that the bike belongs to Sally. The proper noun, *Sally*, is written in a special way to show ownership.

How does a noun show ownership? Read this sentence.

The girl's bike is new.

Because there is only one girl, the noun is singular. Notice the mark between the *l* and the *s*. This mark is called an **apostrophe** ('). You add -*'s* to *girl* to show that the girl has, or owns, the bike.

Look at these nouns that show ownership.

baby's blanket   brother's book
Spot's collar   mother's desk

Is each underlined noun singular? Between which two letters do you find an apostrophe? What does each underlined noun have or own?

Try It Out

For each sentence, tell the singular noun that shows ownership. Then tell what that noun owns or has.

1. We visited Nancy's farm.
2. The horse's stall was filled with hay.
3. The mouse's nest was empty.
4. Who put a bandage on the cow's leg?
5. Mr. Doe's boots were covered with mud.

Most singular nouns show ownership by adding an apostrophe and -*s* (-'s) to the end of the noun.

Written Practice

A. Write each singular noun to show ownership by adding -'*s*.

    1. doctor   **3.** neighbor   **5.** bee   **7.** Mrs. Rosa
    2. robin   **4.** Kelly   **6.** wolf   **8.** puppy

B. To finish each sentence, write a noun that shows ownership. Use the noun in ( ) after each sentence.

    9. Mrs. Cohen read the ____ letter. (teacher)
    10. ____ parents got a letter, too. (Joe)
    11. ____ father went to the school. (Kathy)
    12. He stopped in at the ____ office. (principal)
    13. Mrs. Zaturka shook hands with ____ mother. (Julio)
    14. ____ class drew wall hangings. (Mr. DiCesare)
    15. The teacher showed each ____ art work. (student)
    16. All the parents saw the ____ cage. (hamster)
    17. They all laughed at the ____ funny hop. (rabbit)
    18. Our ____ display was in the library. (club)
    19. Everyone had fun at our ____ open house. (school)

- **Writing Sentences**   Pretend you are showing some friends around your school. Write five sentences telling them about it. Use a noun that shows ownership in each sentence.

7 | Plural Nouns That Show Ownership

You know how to make singular nouns show ownership. You can make plural nouns show ownership, too. Read these sentences.

The <u>boys</u> were playing baseball.
The <u>boys'</u> bats were under the tree.

Look at the underlined nouns. The noun *boys* is plural. Now find the apostrophe. Notice that the apostrophe was written *after* the -*s*. The apostrophe at the end of the word *boys'* tells you that the bats are owned by more than one boy.

Read the sentence below.

The girls' basketball went through the hoop.

Is the noun *girls'* singular or plural? Does the basketball belong to one or more than one girl? The apostrophe at the end of the word tells you that more than one girl owns the basketball.

Try It Out

In each sentence, find the plural noun that shows ownership. Tell where the apostrophe is placed. Then tell what each plural noun owns.

1. My two sisters' room was a mess.
2. The puppies' collars were on the floor.
3. Their friends' books were tossed on the bed.
4. My three brothers' T-shirts were on the chair.
5. Our two neighbors' records were on the dresser.

> Most plural nouns show ownership by adding *only* the apostrophe after the *-s*.

Written Practice

A. Change each plural noun in ( ) to show ownership. Write the new nouns.

1. _____ closet (girls)
2. _____ flags (ships)
3. _____ toys (babies)
4. _____ fur (cats)
5. _____ tools (workers)
6. _____ mother (twins)

B. Write the noun that shows ownership in each sentence below. Write *P* next to each plural noun that shows ownership. Write *S* next to each singular noun that shows ownership.

7. My grandparents' garage is filled with things.
8. My cousins' bikes are there.
9. My family's old baby crib is near the bikes.
10. My aunts' garden hose is in the corner.
11. My uncle's motorcycle is there, too.
12. Where is the puppies' basket?
13. My grandfather's garden tools are in a box.
14. My sisters' books are near the door.
15. My brothers' soccer shoes hang on the wall.
16. Is there room for Grandmother's sports car?

- **Writing Sentences**   Write these plural nouns so that they show ownership. Then write five sentences. Use each plural noun that shows ownership.

friends   dogs   sisters   teachers   sons

8 | Abbreviations

Here is a list of the days of the week and the months of the year. Next to each word is its abbreviation. An **abbreviation** is a short way to write certain words. The names of the months May, June, and July are short. They do not need abbreviations.

Days of the Week		Months of the Year	
Sunday	Sun.	January	Jan.
Monday	Mon.	February	Feb.
Tuesday	Tues.	March	Mar.
Wednesday	Wed.	April	Apr.
Thursday	Thurs.	August	Aug.
Friday	Fri.	September	Sept.
Saturday	Sat.	October	Oct.
		November	Nov.
		December	Dec.

The names of the days of the week and the months of the year are proper nouns. Because they are proper nouns, they must begin with capital letters.

Now look again at the list of abbreviations. Each abbreviation begins with a capital letter and ends with a period. When you are writing sentences, be careful to use whole words, not abbreviations.

Try It Out

Tell what word each abbreviation stands for.

1. Aug. 3. Feb. 5. Dec. 7. Jan. 9. Oct.
2. Sat. 4. Mon. 6. Fri. 8. Thurs. 10. Wed.

▶ An **abbreviation** is a short way of writing a word. Abbreviations usually end with periods. Abbreviations of proper nouns begin with capital letters.

Written Practice

A. For each month below, write the abbreviation.

1. January	**4.** April	**7.** October
2. February	**5.** August	**8.** November
3. March	**6.** September	**9.** December

B. Write the months that do not have abbreviations.

C. Write an abbreviation to answer each question. Remember to begin each abbreviation with a capital letter and end it with a period.

10. Which is your favorite month?
11. What month do you go trick-or-treating?
12. Which day begins the school week?
13. Which weekend day do you like the best?
14. In which month is your favorite holiday?
15. Which day is your favorite?

wrote, written

Look at the underlined words in these sentences.

I <u>wrote</u> a letter.   I have <u>written</u> a letter.
He <u>wrote</u> a note.   He <u>has written</u> a note.

Which word is shown with the helping word *have* or *has*? Which word does not need a helping word?

Use the helping word *has* or *have* with *written*.
Wrote does not need a helping word.

Practice

A. Choose the correct word to complete each sentence.

Last night I (wrote, written) a report. I have (wrote, written) reports often. My friend has (wrote, written) a report, too. I (wrote, written) all about mice.

B. Write the correct word to complete each sentence.

1. Mattie has (wrote, written) me an invitation.
2. She (wrote, written) to say she is having a party.
3. She has (wrote, written) to other friends, too.
4. I have (wrote, written) her a short note.
5. I (wrote, written) that I could hardly wait to come to her party.

did, done

Look at the underlined words in these sentences.

I did my homework.   I have done my homework.
He did his job well.   He has done his job well.

Which word is shown with the helping word *have* or *has*? Which word does not need a helping word?

> Use the helping word *has* or *have* with *done*. *Did* does not need a helping word.

Practice

A. Choose the correct word to complete each sentence.

Derek (did, done) his favorite magic trick for his class. He has (did, done) other tricks for them. He has (did, done) these tricks for three years. When I (did, done) the tricks, they didn't work.

B. Write the correct word to complete each sentence.

1. I (did, done) a handstand in gym class.
2. That was the first time I have (did, done) it right.
3. My friend has (did, done) cartwheels.
4. I have (did, done) them, too.
5. Everyone was surprised when I (did, done) a flip.

- **Writing Sentences**   Write four sentences. Use the words *did*, *done*, *wrote*, and *written*.

Compound Words

The English language is changing and growing. New words are often added to the language. Sometimes two words are put together to make one new word. The new word is called a **compound word**.

The compound word *raincoat* is made up of two words, *rain* and *coat*. Which two words make up each of these compounds?

spaceship   bedtime   sunflower   steamboat

You can tell the meaning of many compound words by looking at their parts. A *room* in which a *class* is held is a *classroom*. What compound word is formed by each pair of underlined words?

the <u>lid</u> over your <u>eye</u>   a <u>plow</u> for moving <u>snow</u>
the <u>time</u> to go to <u>bed</u>   the <u>shell</u> of a <u>sea</u> animal

> ▶ A **compound word** is made up of two words.

Practice

A. To finish each sentence, put together each pair of underlined words and make a compound word.

1. A <u>light</u> that can <u>flash</u> is a ____.
2. A <u>knob</u> on a <u>door</u> is a ____.
3. A <u>paper</u> that is full of <u>news</u> is a ____.

4. <u>Light</u> from the <u>sun</u> is ____.

5. A <u>vine</u> that a <u>grape</u> grows on is a ____.

B. Match one word from the top row to one in the bottom row to make a compound word. Then write new compound words.

ear   foot   play   tooth
ball   ring   brush   ground

C. Tell what two words make up each compound word. Then tell what each compound word means.

  6. horseshoe

  7. housework

  8. sailboat

  9. bookcase

  10. handwriting

  11. playpen

  12. blueberry

  13. airplane

D. Read each sentence. Write the compound words. Then draw a line between the two words that make up each compound. The first one is done for you.

  14. Something in the air says that spring is coming.
  Some / thing

  15. Are the grasshoppers jumping?

  16. Are blackbirds building nests?

  17. Are bullfrogs in the pond?

  18. Is everyone wearing sunglasses?

  19. Are bumblebees buzzing around?

  20. Are skateboards on the sidewalk?

  21. Does the sunlight feel warmer?

  22. Are all the plants outside blooming?

  • **Writing Sentences**   Write five sentences. Use the compound words from exercise C or D.

Review

- **What Are Nouns?** *(pp. 43-44)* Write the nouns in each sentence.

  1. The students went to the museum.
  2. Some girls stared at the old bone.
  3. Some boys watched chickens hatch from eggs.
  4. The children ate their lunches under a tree.
  5. The bus took the students back to the school.

- **Singular and Plural Nouns** *(pp. 45-46)* Look at the nouns you wrote in the exercise above. Write *S* after the nouns that are singular. Write *P* after the nouns that are plural.

- **More Plural Nouns** *(p. 47)* Change the spelling of each singular noun to its plural form. Then write a sentence using each plural noun. Underline the plural noun in your sentence.

  6. story   **7.** cherry   **8.** baby   **9.** puppy

- **Special Plural Nouns** *(pp. 48-49)* Change the underlined noun in each sentence to its plural form.

  10. The man bought the groceries.
  11. The woman made fruit salad.
  12. The child ate the blueberry.
  13. The berry made her tooth turn blue.
  14. They gave their pet mouse some fruit.

- **Common and Proper Nouns** *(pp. 50–51)* Write each noun. Write *C* after each common noun and *P* after each proper noun. Write the proper nouns correctly.

  15. state   **16.** ohio   **17.** country   **18.** canada

- **Nouns That Show Ownership** *(pp. 52–53)* Write the underlined noun in each sentence. Then make it show ownership.

  19. My <u>sister</u> project is in my <u>father</u> workshop.
  20. My <u>brother</u> book is in my <u>grandmother</u> room.
  21. The <u>cat</u> collar and the <u>dog</u> bone are in the box.

- **Plural Nouns That Show Ownership** *(pp. 54–55)* Look at the nouns you wrote in the exercise above. Change these words to plural nouns that show ownership. Then write a sentence using each word.

- **Abbreviations** *(pp. 56–57)* Write the abbreviations.

  22. Saturday   **23.** April   **24.** Monday   **25.** October

- **Using Words Correctly** *(pp. 58–59)* Write the word that completes the sentence.

  My aunt has (wrote, written) a letter to me. She (wrote, written) that she will visit after she has (did, done) her work. I (did, done) *my* work.

- **Building Vocabulary** *(pp. 60–61)* Complete each sentence by making a compound word from the two lists in the box.

	high	walk
	side	road
	rail	way

  26. The train sped by on the ___ track.
  27. There were many cars on the ___.
  28. We often walk to school on the ___.

Maintain

- **Sentences and Word Order** *(pp. 9–11)* For each group of words, write *S* if it is a sentence. Write *NS* if it is not a sentence.

  1. Pam went to the museum with Keith.
  2. Paintings on the wall.
  3. The most beautiful paintings in the museum.
  4. Keith liked the paintings more than Pam did.
  5. The children talked with the guide about the art.

  Using the sentences above, write another sentence for each by changing the word order.

- **Kinds of Sentences and Separating Sentences** *(pp. 12–15, 20–21)* Rewrite the story below by separating the sentences. Then write *S* above each sentence if it is a statement. Write *Q* if it is a question. Write *E* if it is an exclamation.

  Mountain climbing is exciting the climbers have to be very careful look how high the climbers are now have you ever gone mountain climbing

- **Subjects and Predicates** *(pp. 16–19, 43–44)* Write these sentences. Draw a line between the subject and the predicate. Underline the nouns.

  6. The big bear ran through the woods.
  7. The hunter followed the bear.
  8. Many animals live in the forest.
  9. The moonlight shines through the trees.
  10. The stars fill the sky.

- **Singular and Plural Nouns** *(pp. 45–49)* Change each noun to a plural. Write a sentence using each plural noun.

  11. boy   **12.** baby   **13.** teacher   **14.** aunt

- **Nouns That Show Ownership** *(pp. 52–55)* Change each singular noun above to show ownership. Then change each word to a plural noun that shows ownership.

- **Common and Proper Nouns** *(pp. 50–51)* Write each noun. Put a *C* after each common noun. Put a *P* after each proper noun.

  15. Next Monday my brother will take a trip.
  16. Paul will travel to Mexico.
  17. My brother will fly there on a plane.

- **Abbreviations** *(pp. 56–57)* Write the abbreviations for these names of days and months.

  18. Friday **19.** December **20.** Sunday **21.** August

- **Using Words Correctly** *(pp. 22–23, 58–59)* Write the word that completes the sentence.

  Aunt Jen has (wrote, written) Tara a letter. She (wrote, written) to invite her to the city. Tara has (saw, seen) the city before. Tara (went, gone) to visit her. They (did, done) and (saw, seen) many things.

- **Building Vocabulary** *(pp. 60–61)* Complete each sentence by making a compound word from the two lists in the box.

  22. The ____ landed on the flower.
  23. The ____ slowly moved up the river.
  24. She took off her shoes to go ____.

butter	boat
bare	fly
steam	foot

Writing a Paragraph

1 | What Is a Paragraph?

A **paragraph** is a group of sentences that are all about one idea. A paragraph has only one main idea. Each sentence tells something about that idea.

All paragraphs are indented. To indent a paragraph, you leave a space before the first word. Indenting means that a new idea is beginning. Look carefully at the next paragraph.

Do you know how to turn a somersault? First, kneel on the floor. Put your hands on the floor in front of you. Then rest the top of your head on the floor between your hands. Finally, kick up both your legs and bring them all the way over your head.

The main idea of the paragraph above is how to turn a somersault. Do all of the sentences keep to that idea?

Practice

A. Here are some sentences that are all about one idea. Write them as a paragraph. Remember to indent.

What does the word paragraph mean?
Long ago it meant a little mark.
This mark showed where a new idea began.
People made this mark instead of indenting.
Now a paragraph is a group of sentences.

B. Which sentence tells the main idea of the paragraph?

a. Everyone knows what paragraph means.
b. The meaning of paragraph has changed.

2 | Topic Sentences

A **topic sentence** tells the main idea of the paragraph. It tells what the paragraph is about. Usually the topic sentence is the first sentence in the paragraph. Read the paragraph below. The topic sentence is underlined.

Sharpening a pencil is easy. Put the tip of your pencil through the hole in the sharpener. Hold it there firmly while you turn the handle. Soon the handle will turn easily and you will not hear a grinding sound anymore. This means your pencil is sharpened.

- Do all of the sentences in the paragraph fit with the topic sentence?
- What is the main idea of the paragraph?

Practice

Read this paragraph. It does not have a topic sentence. When you have finished reading it, decide what the main idea is. Then make up a good topic sentence.

You can brush all of your top teeth first and then all of your lower teeth. Another way is to brush all of your teeth along the outside. Then open your mouth wider and brush them all on the inner side. You can also brush all the teeth on the right side of your mouth and then all the teeth on the left side.

3 | Order in Paragraphs

Have you ever followed directions for doing something? If so, you know that it is important for the steps to be in order. If they are out of order, you will be confused.

Certain words can help make order clear. *First, next, then,* and *finally* are order words. Look at the way they make the order clear in this paragraph.

If you have a guinea pig, you must clean its cage. First, take the guinea pig out of the cage. Put the guinea pig in a safe place. Next, lift up the old newspaper and wood chips. Throw them away. Spread clean newspaper on the bottom of the cage. Then add a new layer of wood chips. Finally, put the guinea pig back into its clean cage.

- What is the topic sentence of the paragraph?
- What is the main idea?
- Every step does not need to have an order word. How many steps are there in cleaning the cage?

Practice

Below are the steps for a fire drill. The steps are out of order. Write them in order, as a paragraph.

Follow these instructions for a fire drill.
Next, form a straight line.
Leave the room when your teacher tells you to.
First, stand up and push in your chairs.
Walk quickly and quietly outside.

4 | Getting Started

Every day you either hear or give instructions. Giving instructions is telling someone how to do something. If you teach a friend how to play a new game, you are giving instructions. When your parents send you on an errand, they give you instructions. Your teacher often gives instructions.

Your teacher's instructions may sound like this.

Take out a clean sheet of paper.
Put your name at the top.
Answer the questions on page ten.
Then put your paper on my desk.

What would happen if these instructions were out of order? They would not make sense. What would happen if one of these steps was left out? Would you know what to do?

There are two important things to remember when you give instructions.

1. Be sure to tell enough.
2. Tell the steps in order.

Do you know how to peel a banana? Pretend you have met someone who has never peeled a banana. You are going to give this person instructions. Think for a minute about what you will say. Then look on the next page and check your answer with the steps in the box. Do you agree?

How to Peel a Banana

First, take hold of the stem.
Pull it down gently.
Keep pulling until the strip is all the way down.
Then take hold of the next strip at the top.
Pull it down gently.
Do the same with each of the other strips.

Practice

A. Choose one thing to explain to a classmate.

1. how to peel an orange
2. how to make a telephone call
3. how to draw a stick person

Pretend that your classmate has never peeled an orange, made a phone call, or drawn a stick person. Think of all the steps you will need to explain.

B. Tell your instructions to a classmate. Then work together to make your instructions even better.

Steps for Writing Instructions   Here are the steps for writing a paragraph of instructions. You will follow these steps to write your own paragraph.

Step One   Choose a topic.
Step Two   Write your paragraph.
Step Three Revise your paragraph.
Step Four   Proofread your paragraph.
Step Five   Make a final copy to share.

5 | Step One
Choose a Topic

Have you just learned how to do something new? Is there something you could explain to someone?

The students in Brad's class made lists of things they knew how to do. Brad's list looked like this.

weave paper place mats   play Castle

grow a sweet potato vine   get to the library

Brad wondered which topic to write about. He thought it would be better to *show* someone how to weave place mats. Writing about how to get to the school library would be dull. Brad loved to play Castle, but the steps would be too much for one paragraph.

Brad had just grown a sweet potato vine, and he thought someone else might like to try it. He decided to write about how to grow the vine.

Assignment
- Make a List
- Choose a Topic

A. First, make a list of some things you know how to do. Write at least four things on your list.

B. Look at each topic. Ask yourself these questions.

   1. What are the steps?

   2. Can I explain the steps easily in words?

   3. Can I fit the steps into one paragraph?

   4. Which one would I most like to write about?

C. Choose a topic from your list and circle it.

6 | Step Two
Write Your Paragraph

Brad was ready to start writing. He got out paper and a pencil and began his first draft. A **first draft** is the first time you write down your ideas. A first draft can have crossed out words and words that are not spelled correctly. You can go back later and make changes.

Brad's first draft

~~Once I~~ You can grow a long vine from a sweet potato. First, put a sweet potato in a jar make sure the pointed end is down. Then put some water in the jar. Finlly, put the jar in a sunny place. If you wait long enuf, you will have a vine with ~~pret~~ butiful green leaves.

- Did Brad indent his paragraph?
- Are his steps in order? What order words are used?
- Did he tell enough? Could you grow a vine like his?

Assignment • **Write Your First Draft**

Look back at the topic you circled. Think again about all the steps. Then write your first draft. Do not worry about making mistakes. Just get your ideas on paper. If you skip lines when you write, you will have room to make changes later.

7 | Step Three
Revise Your Paragraph

Brad read over his instructions for growing a vine. He saw that he had not indented his paragraph, so he put an arrow at the front to remind him. Then he read his instructions to María.

María said, "I like your idea. I want to try it in my room at home."

"Did I leave anything out?" Brad said.

"I'm not sure," said María. "Should I fill the whole jar with water?"

"No," said Brad, "you should cover just half the potato. You might have to add some water later, too. I must add that to my paragraph."

Brad thanked María for her ideas. Then he made some changes on his paper. Making changes is called **revising.** This is how Brad's paragraph looked after he had revised it.

Brad's revised paragraph

→ ~~Once I~~ You can grow a long vine from a sweet potato. First, put a sweet potato in a jar make sure the pointed end is down. Then put some water in the jar, *so that half the potato is covered* Finlly, put the jar in a sunny place. *Add more water every few days.* If you wait long enuf, you will have a vine with ~~pret~~ butiful green leaves.

- What does Brad's arrow mean?
- How many sentences did Brad change after he talked with María?
- What words did he add?
- Where did he write in his new words?

Assignment
- **Revise Your Paragraph**
- **Discuss Your Paragraph**

A. Read over your instructions. Ask yourself these questions.

1. Is my paragraph indented?
2. Are all my steps in order?
3. What order words have I used to make my steps clear?
4. Have I told enough? Could someone else follow my instructions?

B. Make any changes in your instructions that will make them better. Write your new ideas between the lines, as Brad did.

C. Read your instructions to a classmate. Then discuss them. If your listener has more good ideas, or if you have thought of anything else, make more changes on your paper.

8 | Step Four
Proofread Your Paragraph

You are almost ready to make a final copy of your instructions. You will want to proofread your paragraph before you copy it over. When you **proofread,** you check for mistakes. You make sure all your words are spelled correctly. You make sure that all your sentences start with capital letters. You check to see that all your sentences have an end mark.

Practice

Proofread the sentences below. There are two mistakes in each one. If you are not sure about a spelling, check the dictionary. Write each sentence correctly.

1. nicole and Kevin rote instructions yesterday.
2. Nicole listened to kevin's instructions
3. Did Kevin need to add a few mor steps
4. Ms. garcia said Kevin's writing was clear

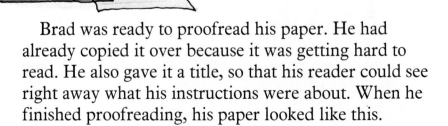

Brad was ready to proofread his paper. He had already copied it over because it was getting hard to read. He also gave it a title, so that his reader could see right away what his instructions were about. When he finished proofreading, his paper looked like this.

Brad's paragraph after proofreading

Growing a Sweet Potato Vine

You can grow a long vine from a sweet potato.
First, put a sweet potato in a jar. M̲ake sure
the pointed end is down. Then put some water
in the jar so that half the potato is covered.
Finally
Fin̶ll̶y, put the jar in a sunny place. Add more
enough
water every few days. If you wait long e̶n̶u̶f̶,
beautiful
you will have a vine with b̶u̶t̶i̶f̶u̶l̶ green leaves.

- Which two sentences were run together? How did
  Brad separate them?
- Where did Brad write correct spellings of words?

Now you are ready to proofread your own paragraph.
On the next page you will find some questions to help
you proofread.

Assignment

• **Proofread Your Paragraph**

Proofread your instructions. Use these proofreading questions to help you.

1. Is my paragraph indented?
2. Did I spell all of my words correctly?

Grammar skills checklist

3. Does each sentence tell a complete thought?
4. Does each sentence begin with a capital letter and end with the right mark?
5. Have I corrected any sentences that run together?
6. Did I use capital letters for proper nouns?

9 | Step Five
Make a Final Copy

Brad took out a clean sheet of paper and copied his paragraph as neatly as he could. Then he thought about how he could share his instructions. He decided that the best way would be to bring in his vine.

Before doing that, he took a large piece of cardboard and pasted his paper with the instructions on it. He pasted another piece of cardboard on the back to make a stand. Then he brought in two things: his vine and an ordinary sweet potato. He set up his instructions next to the potato and the potato vine to make a display.

Assignment

- **Make a Final Copy**
- **Share Your Instructions**

A. Copy your paragraph over as neatly as you can.
B. Make up a good title and write it at the top.
C. Read over your paragraph again to make sure you have not made any mistakes.
D. Think of a way to share your instructions.

- You can make a poster showing the steps.
- You can use pictures of before and after.
- You can make a display as Brad did.

Verbs

1 | What Is a Verb?

You have learned that a noun is a word that names a person, place, or thing. What is the noun in each sentence below?

The girl runs.
The girl rides.
The girl swims.

The noun in each sentence is the same. Each sentence tells about the girl. What does the girl do in the first sentence? What does she do in the next sentence? What does she do in the last sentence?

The words *runs*, *rides*, and *swims* tell what the girl does. These words are called verbs. **Verbs** tell what someone or something does. We say that verbs show action. Read the sentence below. What is the verb in this sentence?

Ellen kicks the ball.

The word *kicks* is the verb because it tells what Ellen does. *Kicks* shows the action in the sentence.

In the sentence below, there is a line between the subject and the predicate. The subject of the sentence tells who or what the sentence is about. The predicate tells what the subject does or is. What is the verb in the sentence below? Is the verb in the subject or in the predicate?

Hank / pitches the ball.

The verb *pitches* is in the predicate. The verb is always part of the predicate.

Try It Out

A. Read each sentence. Tell what the verb is.

1. Gilbert's dog chases cars.
2. Joan planted a seed.
3. The sun shines.
4. The children built a birdhouse.
5. Squirrels hide their nuts.
6. Lightning flashed in the night sky.
7. The waves crash on the beach.
8. The jet roared.
9. Robin hung her picture on the wall.
10. Terry whistled clearly.
11. The baby cries.
12. A snail crawls slowly.
13. José bumped the desk.
14. Rhonda carries the papers.
15. The leaves fell to the ground.

B. Think of two verbs. Share them with the class.

> ▶ A **verb** is a word that shows action.

Written Practice

A. Write each sentence. Put a line between the subject and the predicate. Then underline the verb. The first one has been done for you.

1. The crowd cheered the players.
   The crowd / <u>cheered</u> the players.
2. Sharon swims every Saturday.
3. The elephant sprayed water with its trunk.
4. The monkey danced to the music.
5. Clouds drift slowly across the sky.
6. The kitten jumps playfully.

B. Think of a verb that would make sense in each sentence. Write your sentences.

7. Luke _____ down the street.
8. The bird _____.
9. Ronald _____ for his lost jacket.
10. The girl _____ loudly.
11. The horse _____ in the field.
12. Bill _____ the door.
13. Andy _____ the milk.
14. Amanda _____ her bike.
15. The children _____.
16. Sam _____ the book on the table.

- **Writing Sentences**   Write five sentences about a game. Underline the verbs.

2 | Verbs in the Present

Verbs show the action in sentences. They tell you what is happening. Verbs also can tell you the time of the action. When an action is happening right now, we say it is in the **present time**. Read the sentence below.

Jill sleds down the hill.

What is Jill doing? When is Jill sledding? The verb *sleds* tells that the action is happening in the present.

Verbs in the present have two forms. The correct form to use depends on the subject of the sentence. If the subject is singular, the verb ends with *-s*. If the subject is plural, the verb does not end with *-s*. Read these sentences.

Susan wins the prize.
The boys win the prize.

Which sentence has a singular subject? How does the verb end? Which sentence has a plural subject? How does the verb end?

Try It Out

Tell the correct verb form for each sentence.

1. Snowflakes (fall, falls) quietly.
2. Paul and Toby (love, loves) the snow.
3. Toby (get, gets) the sled.
4. The boys (race, races) to the hill.
5. Their mother (take, takes) their picture.

> ▶ Verbs in the **present time** tell that an action is happening now. With a singular subject, verbs in the present end with -*s*. With a plural subject, verbs in the present do not end with -*s*.

Written Practice

Write the correct verb for each sentence. Then write *S* if the subject is singular. Write *P* if the subject is plural.

1. Animals (move, moves) in different ways.
2. Rabbits (hop, hops) into bushes.
3. Snakes (wiggle, wiggles) in the grass.
4. Chipmunks (scampers, scamper) over rocks.
5. The hippo (stand, stands) in the lake.
6. The horse (gallop, gallops).
7. Some bears (climb, climbs) trees.
8. Monkeys (swings, swing) on branches.
9. The duck (dives, dive) under the water.
10. A snail (crawl, crawls).

• **Writing Sentences**   Write five sentences about animals. Use the verbs below.

11. hears   12. eat   13. jump   14. lives   15. run

3 | More Verbs in the Present

Most verbs in the present end with *-s* when used with a singular subject. For some verbs, you need to add *-es* rather than *-s*. Read the pairs of sentences below.

The boys guess answers.　　The girls fish.
Larry guesses answers.　　The girl fishes.
Teachers watch us.　　　　The painters mix paint.
The coach watches us.　　　Joy mixes paint.

The verbs *guess, fish, watch,* and *mix* add the ending *-es*. Whenever you use a singular subject with a verb that ends with *-s, -sh, -ch,* or *-x*, add *-es* instead of *-s*.
Read the sentences below.

The students carry books.　　The kites fly high.
Marvin carries books.　　　 The kite flies high.

Look at the verb in each pair of sentences. The spelling of the verbs *carry* and *fly* changes when used with singular subjects. The *y* changes to *i*. Then the ending *-es* is added. Whenever a verb ends with a consonant and *-y*, change the *y* to *i* before adding *-es*.

Try It Out

Read each sentence. Spell the present form for each verb in ( ). The first one has been done for you.

1. Tammy ____ the broken toy. (fix)　　**fixes**
2. Father ____ the food. (pass)
3. Alan ____ about his lost dog. (worry)
4. The sailor ____ on a star. (wish)

5. The meat _____ in the pan. (fry)
6. Willa _____ Ramón to dive. (teach)

Verbs in the present that end with -*s*, -*sh*, -*ch*, or
-*x* add -*es* when used with singular subjects.
Verbs in the present that end with a consonant
and -*y* change the *y* to *i* and add -*es*.

Written Practice

A. Read each sentence. Write the correct verb form.

1. Mr. Hogan (teach, teaches) at Taft School.
2. The students (study, studies) very hard.
3. The teacher (work, works) with each group.
4. The students (copy, copies) from the chalkboard.
5. Matt (finish, finishes) first.

B. Write the present form of each verb in ( ).

6. Maria _____ to the house. (hurry)
7. Sandy _____ her some hot soup. (fix)
8. The rain _____ on the street. (splash)
9. Maria _____ out by the fireplace. (stretch)
10. The machine _____ her clothes. (dry)

- **Writing Sentences**   Write three sentences. In
each one, use the present form of the verb *touch*,
pass, or *carry*. Use a singular subject with each verb.

More Verbs in the Present   **87**

4 | Verbs in the Past

Verbs can tell you that an action is happening in the present. Verbs also can tell you that an action happened in the past. Read the sentences below the pictures.

Judy opens the box.   Judy opened the box.

Which picture shows that Judy is opening the box now? The verb *opens* shows the present time. In the second picture, Judy has already opened the box. When an action has already happened, we say that it is in the **past time**. The verb *opened* is in the past time. It ends with *-ed*.

Many verbs show past time by adding the ending *-ed*. Look at the way these verbs change to past time by adding *-ed*.

PRESENT: kick   float   rock   follow
PAST: kicked   floated   rocked   followed

Try It Out

A. Tell the verb that shows past time.

1. Jerry (rows, rowed) the boat.
2. The boat (passes, passed) two ducks.

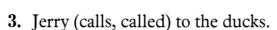

3. Jerry (calls, called) to the ducks.
4. The ducks (quacked, quack) loudly.
5. Jerry (enjoyed, enjoys) the sound.

B. Tell the past form for each verb.

6. play **7.** turn **8.** talk **9.** join

> ▶ Verbs in the **past time** show that an action has already happened. Many verbs show past time by adding *-ed*.

Written Practice

A. Write each verb. Write *present* if the verb shows present time. Write *past* if the verb shows past time.

1. The campers cook over the campfire.
2. They walked for hours today.
3. Molly laughed at the funny joke.
4. The children talked to the clown.
5. Carlos fixed a ham sandwich.
6. Ricky watches the children on Saturday.
7. The crabgrass filled the vegetable garden.
8. Jody weeds the garden every week.

B. Write the past time of these verbs.

9. climb **10.** work **11.** mix **12.** splash **13.** look

• **Writing Sentences** Write five sentences. Use the verbs you wrote in exercise B.

5 | More Verbs in the Past

Most verbs show past time just by adding the ending -ed. However, if a verb ends with -e, drop the -e before adding -ed. Look at the way these verbs change.

race + ed = raced   joke + ed = joked

When a verb ends with a consonant and -y, change the y to i before adding -ed. *Cry* changes to *cried*.

cr$\overset{i}{\cancel{y}}$ + ed = cried

Try It Out

Change these verbs to past time. Spell each word.

1. change   3. wipe   5. copy   7. chase
2. reply   4. trade   6. dry   8. surprise

Verbs ending with -e drop the final -e and add -ed to show past time. Verbs ending with a consonant and -y change the y to i and add -ed.

Written Practice

Write the past time of each verb.

1. smile   3. fry   5. score   7. invite
2. name   4. rake   6. study   8. marry

- **Writing Sentences**   Write five sentences in the past time. Use verbs from the list above.

6 | Special Verbs

Some verbs do not show action. They do not add the endings -*s* or -*ed*. Read the sentences below. Look at the verb in each sentence.

> I am happy.
> The dog is hungry.
> You are my friend.
> Susan was the winner.
> The children were late for school.

The verbs *am*, *is*, *are*, *was*, and *were* are special. Sometimes these verbs are difficult to use correctly. They do not follow the rules you have learned for other verbs. Because you use these verbs often, it is important to know how to use them correctly.

Am, *is*, and *are* show present time. *Was* and *were* show past time. The chart shows when to use each verb.

Subject	Present	Past
I	am	was
you	are	were
he/she/it	is	was
singular noun (John)	is	was
we	are	were
they	are	were
plural noun (dogs)	are	were

Try It Out

A. Tell which special verb to use with each subject. Use the verb that shows present time.

1. I   4. The boat   7. She
2. We   5. You   8. Troy and Krista
3. Jeff   6. The balloons   9. Emily

B. Tell which special verb to use with each subject. Use the verb that shows past time.

10. You   13. He   16. The rabbits
11. They   14. The book   17. We
12. Janet   15. A cow and a calf   18. I

> *Am*, *are*, *is*, *was*, and *were* are special verbs. They do not take the endings *-s* or *-ed*.

Written Practice

A. Write the correct verb for each sentence.

1. I (is, am) in Mrs. Schultz's class.
2. The students (are, is) in the auditorium.
3. We (are, is) excited about the reports.
4. You (was, were) in the last row.
5. Ted and Wilfred (were, was) in the program.
6. Lisa (were, was) the class reporter yesterday.
7. The camel (is, are) the topic of Lisa's report.
8. Camels (are, is) her favorite animals.
9. Jane and Kevin (is, are) the reporters today.
10. You (was, were) a good reporter, too.

B. Each sentence is written in the present time. Change the verb to show past time. Write the new verb. The first one is done for you.

11. Frank is a roller skater.   **was**
12. We are members of a club.
13. The members are good skaters.
14. You are the best skater.
15. I am early for every lesson.
16. Ms. Ames is our teacher.

● **Writing Sentences** Use each word as the subject of a sentence. Write the sentences in the present time. Use the correct special verbs.

17. I   **18.** You   **19.** Puppies   **20.** Pam

Use each word as the subject of a sentence. Write the sentences in past time. Use the correct special verbs.

21. Games   **22.** We   **23.** Tim   **24.** I

7 | Contractions with *not*

Sometimes two words are put together and shortened to make one word. Read these sentences.

> I do not like rainy days.
> I don't like rainy days.

The verb *do* and the word *not* were put together and shortened to make the word *don't*. *Don't* is called a **contraction**. The letter *o* was dropped from *not* to form the contraction. An apostrophe (') was put in place of the dropped *o*.

Many contractions are made by putting together a verb and the word *not*. Read this list.

is not	isn't	did not	didn't
are not	aren't	do not	don't
was not	wasn't	does not	doesn't
were not	weren't	could not	couldn't
have not	haven't	should not	shouldn't
had not	hadn't	would not	wouldn't
has not	hasn't	cannot	can't

Sometimes more than one letter is dropped to make a contraction. What letters were dropped from *cannot* to form *can't*?

The contraction *won't* is special. Read these sentences.

> The robins will not eat the birdseed.
> The robins won't eat the birdseed.

What two words are put together to make the contraction *won't*? You must change the spelling of *will* and leave out the *o* in *not* to make *won't*.

Try It Out

Find the contraction in each sentence. Tell the two words put together to make the contraction.

1. The television wasn't working.
2. We didn't know what was wrong with it.
3. It couldn't be fixed today.
4. It can't be fixed this week.
5. We won't see the program about whales.

▶ A **contraction** is one word made by putting two words together and shortening them. Put an apostrophe (') in place of any letters dropped to make the contraction.

Written Practice

A. Write the contraction for each pair of words.

1. do not	4. could not	7. does not
2. were not	5. was not	8. did not
3. will not	6. are not	9. have not

B. Write the two words put together to make each contraction below.

10. wouldn't	13. hadn't	16. won't
11. doesn't	14. didn't	17. weren't
12. isn't	15. don't	18. aren't

- **Writing Sentences** Write five sentences about something that is broken. Use five contractions from exercise B.

ran, run

Look at the underlined words in these sentences.

I ran a race.   I have run a race.
He ran a race.   He has run a race.

The sentences on the left show that *ran* needs no helping word. The ones on the right use *have* or *has* with *run*.

> Use the helping word *has* or *have* with *run*. *Ran* does not need a helping word.

Practice

A. Choose the correct word to complete each sentence.

Chris (ran, run) down the street. The other racers (ran, run) behind her. Janet (run, ran) almost as fast as Chris. Janet could have (ran, run) faster. She has (ran, run) faster in other races.

B. Write the correct word to complete each sentence.

1. The puppy Boner (ran, run) after Daisy, the cat.
2. Daisy (run, ran) up a tree.
3. Daisy has (run, ran) from Boner other times.
4. Boner and Daisy have (run, ran) from Bruiser.

- **Writing Sentences** Write two sentences using *ran* correctly. Then write three sentences using *run*.

came, come

Look at the underlined words in these sentences.

I <u>came</u> to visit.   I have <u>come</u> to visit.
She <u>came</u> to visit.   She <u>has come</u> to visit.

The sentences on the left show that *came* needs no helping word. The ones on the right use *have* or *has* with *come*.

> Use the helping word *has* or *have* with *come*.
> *Came* does not need a helping word.

Practice

A. Choose the correct word to complete each sentence.

Officer Jack Coakley (came, come) to our school. He (came, come) to tell us about safety rules. He has (came, come) to speak to us before. This time he has (come, came) with a film on bicycle safety. Each class (come, came) to see the program.

B. Write the correct word to complete each sentence.

1. The robin has (came, come) to Lori's yard.
2. It (came, come) to build a nest.
3. It has (come, came) back for two years.
4. The robin (come, came) earlier this year than last.
5. Lori's family (came, come) to see the nest.
6. Lori's friends have (came, come), too.

- **Writing Sentences**   Write five sentences about a visitor. Use *came* in two sentences. Use *come* in the other three.

9 Building Vocabulary

Prefixes

A **prefix** can be added to the beginning of some words to make new words. Look at these examples.

un + happy = unhappy   re + tell = retell

Un- and *re-* are prefixes. A prefix changes the meaning of the word it is added to. If you know what the prefix means, you can understand the new word.

The prefix *un-* means "not." The word *unhappy* means "not happy." The prefix *re-* means "again." The word *retell* means "tell again."

▸ A **prefix** is added to the beginning of some words.

Practice

A. Give the meaning of each word.

1. unkind   **2.** replay   **3.** unfair   **4.** remake

B. Add *un-* or *re-* to the word in ( ) to fit each blank.

5. A jar that is not covered is ____. (covered)
6. Lorna named her dog again. She ____ it. (named)
7. Steve ____ the package to see inside. (tied)

• **Writing Sentences**   Write four sentences. Use words from exercise A.

Suffixes

A **suffix** can be added to the end of some words to make new words. Look at these examples.

farm + er = farmer   fear + less = fearless

The endings -*er* and -*less* are suffixes. Like a prefix, a suffix changes the meaning of the word it is added to.

The suffix -*er* means "a person or thing who does something." A farmer is a person who farms. The suffix -*less* means "without." The word *fearless* means "without fear."

> ▶ A **suffix** is added to the end of some words.

Practice

A. Give the meaning of each word.

1. hopeless   **3.** baker   **5.** rider
2. singer   **4.** useless   **6.** joyless

B. Complete each sentence. Use a word that has the suffix -*er* or -*less*.

7. A person who speaks is a ____.
8. A doll without hair is ____.
9. A person who leads a group is a ____.
10. The sky without a cloud is ____.
11. The stray kitten is without a home. It is ____.
12. A person who paints is a ____.

• **Writing Sentences**   Write five sentences. Use words from exercise A.

Review

- **What Is a Verb?** *(pp. 81–83)* Write each sentence. Put a line between the subject and predicate. Draw one line under the verb.

  1. The dog, Buff, dashed after a rabbit.
  2. Buff ran too far from home.
  3. Joanne and Jessie searched for Buff.
  4. Buff heard their secret whistle.

- **Verbs in the Present** *(pp. 84–85)* Write the correct verb for each sentence.

  5. A bee (land, lands) on a flower.
  6. Pollen (stick, sticks) on the bee's legs.
  7. The bees (takes, take) the pollen to the hive.

- **More Verbs in the Present** *(pp. 86–87)* Write the correct verb for each sentence.

  8. Ned and Jim (carries, carry) the ladder.
  9. Jim (pass, passes) the paint to Susan.
  10. Dad (fix, fixes) the broken window.
  11. Susan and Ned (finishes, finish) their work first.
  12. Ned (touch, touches) the wet paint.

- **Verbs in the Past** *(pp. 88–89)* Write the word in ( ) in past time to complete each sentence.

  13. Roland and April ____ into the boat. (climb)
  14. The waves ____ against the boat. (splash)
  15. The children ____ for whales. (watch)

- **More Verbs in the Past** *(p. 90)* Write the past time of each verb.

  16. study   **18.** waste   **20.** bake   **22.** hike
  17. trace   **19.** cry   **21.** carry   **23.** reply

- **Special Verbs** *(pp. 91–93)* Write the correct verb for each sentence.

  24. The baskets (were, was) full of fruit.
  25. My father (are, is) a teacher.
  26. I (is, am) the winner of the contest.
  27. We (are, is) writing a secret message.

- **Contractions with** *not* *(pp. 94–95)* Write the contraction for each pair of words.

  28. do not   **30.** have not   **32.** was not
  29. cannot   **31.** should not   **33.** will not

- **Using Words Correctly** *(pp. 96–97)* Write the correct word to complete each sentence.

  34. Gary's friends have (come, came) to watch him race.
  35. Gary has (ran, run) in many races.
  36. Gary (ran, run) two miles in twenty minutes.
  37. He (come, came) in second.

- **Building Vocabulary** *(pp. 98–99)* Write the meaning of each underlined word.

  38. The sailors worked to <u>rebuild</u> the boat.
  39. A <u>careless</u> worker lost his hammer.
  40. The <u>worker</u> looked everywhere for the hammer.
  41. An <u>unknown</u> person found the hammer.

Writing a Descriptive Paragraph

1 | Using Your Senses

Every single day you use all of your five senses—seeing, hearing, smelling, touching, and tasting. Most of the time you do not think very much about them, but they are always there. Stop for a minute, and think about how you used your five senses so far today. What did you see? What did you hear? What did you smell? touch? taste?

Did any words come into your mind when you asked yourself those questions? Words like *shiny, loud, soft,* and *light* are **sense words.** They help you describe what you see and hear and touch.

Here are some sense words.

Color	Size and Shape	Sound
red	round	hum
light green	tiny	bang
gray	pointed	clang

Smell	Touch	Taste
fresh	smooth	bitter
fishy	bumpy	sweet
smoky	soft	spicy

Practice

You could add lots of words to the chart. Use your five senses to think of some of them. Then write the headings *Color, Size and Shape, Sound, Smell, Touch,* and *Taste* on your paper. Write your own list of words under each heading. Share your lists with your class.

2 | Using Exact Words

Read these sentences. Which sentence gives a clearer picture?

The girl <u>went</u> across the street.
The girl <u>skipped</u> across the street.

Skipped gives a more exact picture than *went*. It tells you just how the girl moved. The word *skipped* makes the second sentence clear.

If you want to tell a friend about your new kitten, how will you describe it? What if you say it is a *nice* kitten? What picture will your friend have? What if you say it is a *pretty* kitten? Will the picture be any clearer? What if you say it is a *little black* kitten *with fluffy fur*? Then your friend will have a much better picture of your kitten.

Practice

Rewrite each sentence below. Change the underlined word to a more exact word. Use the words in the box to help you.

1. The apple tasted <u>good</u>.
2. The flowers are <u>red</u>.
3. The kitten's fur is <u>nice</u>.
4. Jason <u>went</u> after the ball.
5. The <u>bad</u> weather lasted for a week.

| soft |
| sweet |
| raced |
| stormy |
| roses |

3 | Getting Started

Imagine that you are painting a picture of your best friend. You use colors to show what you see. If you wrote about your friend, you would use words to show what you see. The word pictures that you write are called **descriptions.**

Practice

Look around your classroom. Pick one thing that you can describe. Using your five senses, think of all the words that would describe it. Then describe it to someone. Make your words paint a picture of it in your listener's mind.

Steps for Writing a Description Here are the steps for writing a description. You will follow these steps to write your own description.

Step One Choose a topic.
Step Two Write your description.
Step Three Revise your description.
Step Four Proofread your description.
Step Five Make a final copy to share.

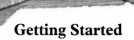

4 | Step One
Choose a Topic

Think of all the things, places, or people you could describe. Which one will you write about? Would you like to describe a favorite toy or a pet? Is there a special place or person you want to describe?

Nina made this list of ideas for her description.

the pillow I made   my town

my dog Cheeser   my house

Nina looked over her list. She decided that there was too much to say about her town for one paragraph. Nina loved her house. She thought of something to say about every single room. It was too much, too. Nina decided to write about either her pillow or Cheeser. After thinking some more, she chose Cheeser.

Assignment
- **Make a List**
- **Choose a Topic**

A. What are the special things or people you would like to describe? Make a list of your ideas. Then ask yourself these questions.

   1. Which one can I describe best?
   2. Which is the best one for using sense words?
   3. Which one would I like most to write about?

B. Decide what you want to describe. Be sure you can picture it clearly in your mind. Circle that topic on your paper.

C. Draw a picture of what you are going to describe.

5 | Step Two
Write Your Description

Think carefully about what you are going to describe. Look at it before you write, if you can. Look hard, and try to see everything about it. Use your senses of smell, sound, touch, and taste.

In your first draft, you just want to get your ideas on paper. You can add words or cross them out. Your first draft is not supposed to be perfect.

Here is Nina's first draft. Notice that Nina made some mistakes.

Nina's first draft

My dog's name is Cheeser. He is furry and has a big tail. He ~~can~~ loves to fetch sticks, Cheeser is the best dog I know

- Did Nina paint a clear picture of Cheeser?
- Did she use words that describe color, size, shape, sound, smell, or touch?

Assignment • Write Your First Draft

Look again at the picture you drew. Then write the first draft of your description. You may want to skip a line as you write. That way you will have room to make changes.

6 | Step Three
Revise Your Description

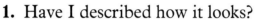

For the first time, your description is on paper. Now you can look for ways to make it better. Think again about the person or place or thing you described. Then look back at your paper, and ask yourself these questions.

1. Have I described how it looks?
2. Have I described how it sounds?
3. Have I described how it smells?
4. Have I described how it tastes?
5. Have I described what it feels like to touch?
6. Have I used exact words?

Using these questions gave Nina some new ideas. She could not use the question about taste for Cheeser, but she could use all the others.

Nina wanted someone else to hear her description, too. She wanted to check that it gave a clear picture of Cheeser. She read her description to Bobby. She asked him whether he could get a picture of Cheeser from what she had written.

Bobby said that he could not tell whether Cheeser was big or little. He asked Nina to tell him more about Cheeser. When they had finished talking, Nina had a much better idea of what she wanted to say. She knew she could do a better job now. She decided to start her description all over again.

Nina also thought of a title for her paper. She wrote it at the top of the page. She used capital letters to begin the first word and every important word in the title.

Read Nina's new description on the next page carefully.

Nina's new description

My Playful Mutt

My dog's name is Cheeser. He is a mutt, but he looks like a big collie. He has a furry head and funny floppy ears. ^shaggy his tail ^wags moves when he is happy. His ruf tung licks my face. He always smells like wet leaves When he wants to play, he is very noisey ^barks loudly. He loves to fetch sticks, Cheeser is the ^most playful best dog I know

- Look at Nina's first draft on page 107. Do you learn more about Cheeser in the first draft or in Nina's new description? What new things about Cheeser has she added?
- How many of the five senses did she use in her first draft?
- How many of the senses did she use in her new description?
- Nina made some other changes as she wrote her new description. What words did she change into more exact words?

Assignment

- Revise Your Description
- Discuss Your Description

A. Read your description to yourself. Have you used your five senses? Ask yourself the questions on page 108. Make a mark on your paper to show where you can add something to give a better picture.

B. Now read your description once more. This time look for places to use more exact words.

C. Now make changes in your description. Add new ideas. Cross out words that are not exact, and write better words above them. If you want to, write your description over to make it better, like Nina did.

D. Read your description with the changes to someone—a classmate or your teacher. Discuss with your listener how to make it better. Then make more changes if you like your listener's ideas or if you have thought of anything else.

7 | Proofread Your Description

Now you are ready to look more closely at your description. Is each word spelled correctly? Are capital letters, commas, periods, and apostrophes used correctly? Checking your writing for mistakes is called **proofreading.**

Nina thought her description looked messy, so she copied it over. Then she proofread it.

Nina's description after proofreading

> ## My Playful Mutt
>
> My dog's name is Cheeser. He is a mutt, but he looks like a big collie. He has a furry head and floppy ears. His shaggy tail wags when he is happy. His ruf tung licks my face. He always smells like wet leaves When he wants to play, he barks loudly. He loves to fetch sticks, Cheeser is the most playful dog I know

(annotations: H above "his"; rough tongue above "ruf tung")

- What end marks did Nina add?
- Which words were misspelled?
- Where did she add a capital letter?

Practice

Before you check your own writing, proofread these sentences. Each sentence has two mistakes. Write each sentence correctly. If you are not sure of how to spell a word, look it up.

1. steven described his balloon
2. It was perple
3. it made a loud pop when it broke

Assignment • **Proofread Your Description**

Now you are ready to proofread your description. Ask yourself these questions.

1. Is my paragraph indented?
2. Did I spell all of my words correctly?

Grammar skills checklist

3. Does each sentence tell a complete thought?
4. Does each sentence begin with a capital letter and end with the right mark?
5. Have I corrected any sentences that run together?
6. Did I use capital letters for proper nouns?
7. Have I used apostrophes correctly to show ownership?

8 | Step Five
Make a Final Copy

Nina copied over her description carefully. Then she thought of a way to make her paragraph look special. She took a large piece of light brown construction paper. She pasted her description to the center of it. Nina drew a shaggy tail near the right-hand edge. She drew Cheeser's face near the left-hand edge. She made four legs at the bottom of the paper.

Then Nina found some photographs of Cheeser. She taped the best ones along the sides of the brown paper. She was ready to share her description and pictures with the class. Here is how it looked.

Assignment
- **Make a Final Copy**
- **Share Your Description**

A. Copy your paragraph in your best handwriting.
B. Read your description one last time. Be sure that you have not made a mistake in copying.
C. Think of a special way to share your description.

- You can attach your drawing to your paragraph.
- You can make a new drawing.
- You can combine photographs and drawings to display your work, as Nina did.

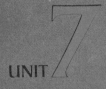

UNIT 7 Pronouns

1 | What Are Pronouns?

You have learned that a noun can name a person, a place, or a thing. Find the nouns in the sentence below.

Kim and José visited a room with mirrors.

Kim, *José*, *room*, and *mirrors* are nouns. *Kim* and *José* are proper nouns. *Room* and *mirrors* are common nouns.
Now read these two sentences.

José looked into the mirror.
He could not believe his eyes.

Find the noun in the first sentence. Now read the second sentence again. What word takes the place of José in this sentence?
The word *He* is used in place of the proper noun *José*. The word *He* is a pronoun. A **pronoun** is a word that takes the place of a noun in a sentence. Look at the chart below. All the words in this chart are pronouns.

Singular	Plural
I	we
you	you
he	they
she	
it	

Pronouns can be singular or plural. Look again at the chart. Which pronouns are singular? Which pronouns are plural? Which pronoun can be either singular or plural?

Read the sentences below. Find the singular pronoun in each pair of sentences. Which noun does each pronoun replace?

Todd made orange juice. He read the directions.
Kerry was thirsty. She drank the juice.
The juice was cold. It tasted good.

Look at the pronoun in each sentence below. Which pronouns are singular? Which one is plural?

I was late.
You were the only person here.
You boys are late, too.

The pronoun *you* in the second sentence is singular. In the third sentence, *you* is plural.

Read each pair of sentences below. Find the plural pronouns. Which words does each pronoun replace?

Susan and I worked hard. We were tired.
The students can help. They are ready.

Try It Out

Find the pronouns in these sentences. Tell if they are singular or plural.

1. Last night we had a blizzard.
2. I could hear the wind blowing.
3. It was howling.
4. They watched the snow fall all day.
5. We could not go to school.
6. She could hardly wait to go skiing.
7. You are wearing a blue ski vest.
8. He wanted to read by the fire.
9. We will have an extra vacation day.

> ▶ A **pronoun** is a word used in place of a noun or nouns.
>
> *I*, *you*, *he*, *she*, *it*, *we*, and *they* are pronouns.

Written Practice

A. Write the pronoun in each sentence. Then write *S* if it is singular or *P* if it is plural.

1. Ted and I went fishing.
2. He left Fifi ashore.
3. She barked for hours.
4. She swam to the boat.
5. It almost tipped over.
6. Ted and I caught two bass.
7. They were too small.
8. We threw the fish back.
9. Did you have more luck?

B. Write a pronoun to replace the underlined part of each sentence.

10. Dan is a good sailor.
11. Jill likes to sail, too.
12. The boat has one sail.
13. Two people can handle the sail.
14. The sailors will have a good afternoon.
15. Dan watched the clouds.
16. The wind filled the sail with air.
17. Tammy and I smiled as they sailed away.

- **Writing Sentences** Write five sentences, using a different pronoun from the chart on page 115. Write about what you and your friends like to do.

What Are Pronouns? 117

2 | More Pronouns

You know that the words *I, you, she, he, it, we,* and *they* are pronouns. There are other pronouns, too. Look at the chart below. Which of these pronouns are singular? Which are plural?

Singular	Plural
me	us
him	them
her	

Each of the pronouns in the chart can take the place of a noun. Read these two sentences.

Fern cooks dinner with <u>Russell</u>.
Fern cooks dinner with <u>him</u>.

What are the nouns in the first sentence? *Fern, dinner,* and *Russell* are the nouns. What pronoun takes the place of *Russell* in the second sentence? The pronoun *him* takes the place of the proper noun Russell.

Read the sentences below. Can you find the pronouns in these sentences?

Does Sharon want to paint with <u>me</u>?
Ben can join <u>us</u>.
Let <u>him</u> use the thin brushes.
Ted can help <u>her</u> clean up.
Show these beautiful paintings to <u>them</u>.

Try It Out

Find the pronoun in each sentence.

1. Aunt Rita made a chicken dinner for us.
2. The family thanked her for the meal.
3. Joe helped me wash the dishes.
4. Bill will help him.
5. Mom watched them proudly.

Other pronouns that take the place of nouns are
me, *him*, *her*, *us*, and *them*.

Written Practice

In each sentence below, change the underlined word or words to a pronoun. Write the new sentences. The first one is done for you.

1. Let's go watch the teams.
   Let's go watch them.
2. You go with Anne.
3. I invited Bill, too.
4. A goal was kicked by Wendy.
5. Who else kicked goals?
6. We all cheered for the players.
7. The players thanked the coaches.

- **Writing Sentences**   Write five sentences, using a different pronoun in each sentence. Choose from the pronouns below.

me   you   him   her   it   us   you   them

3 | *I* and *me*

You often use the pronouns *I* and *me* when you speak and write.

I left a message for Nat.
Nat called me right back.

How do you know when to use *I* and when to use *me*? Look at these sentences below.

Subject	Predicate
Randy and I	dived into the pool.
The lifeguard	watched Randy and me.

Notice that *I* is used in the subject of the first sentence. You should use the pronoun *I* only in the subject of your sentences. Do not use *I* in the predicate.

Read the second sentence again. Notice that the pronoun *me* is used in the predicate. You should use *me* only in the predicate of your sentences. Do not use *me* in the subject.

If you have trouble choosing between *I* and me , try this test. Say the sentence with only *I* or *me*, leaving out the other noun.

Lil and I talked to Jim. Jim walked with Lil and me.
I talked to Jim. Jim walked with me.

Now look back at the sentences that name *Randy* or *Lil* and *I* or *me*. Notice that *I* and *me* are always the last of the names given. Whenever you speak of yourself and another person, it is polite to name yourself last.

Try It Out

Read each sentence. Choose the correct pronoun for each sentence. Tell whether the pronoun is in the subject or the predicate.

1. Rob and (I, me) helped Dad in the yard.
2. Dad gave Rob and (I, me) rakes.
3. Rob and (I, me) raked the leaves into a pile.
4. The wind blew the leaves toward Rob and (I, me).
5. Rob and (I, me) worked hard all day.

> When you speak of yourself, use *I* in the subject of the sentence. Use *me* in the predicate. Whenever you speak of yourself and another person, it is polite to name yourself last.

Written Practice

Write these sentences. Use *I* or *me*. Remember to use *I* in the subject and *me* in the predicate.

1. Val, Jon, and _____ baked bread.
2. Val gave Jon and _____ the flour.
3. Jon and _____ took turns helping.
4. The oven was near Val and _____.
5. Kim asked Val and _____ for a slice of bread.
6. Kim and _____ tasted the hot bread.
7. Val gave _____ the recipe.
8. Kim and _____ will make bread next week.

- **Writing Sentences**   Write five sentences that name yourself and another person. Use *I* in three of your sentences. Use *me* in the other two sentences.

4 | Contractions

You know that a contraction is a word that is made up of two words joined together. A letter or letters are left out of one of the words. An apostrophe is written in place of the missing letter or letters. Here are some contractions you have learned. They are verbs used with the word *not*.

hasn't   don't   isn't   won't

Some contractions are made by using a pronoun and a verb. Below is a list of some of these contractions. Which pronouns begin these contractions? Which letters are left out?

I am = I'm   she will = she'll
you are = you're   we will = we'll
he is = he's   they will = they'll
she is = she's   I have = I've
it is = it's   you have = you've
we are = we're   he has = he's
they are = they're   she has = she's
I will = I'll   it has = it's
you will = you'll   we have = we've
he will = he'll   they have = they've

Try It Out

Find the contraction in each sentence below.

1. You've heard the good news.
2. We're off to Florida.
3. They'll meet us in Miami.
4. He's ready to go!

> A contraction can be made by joining a pronoun and a verb. Use an apostrophe in place of the letter or letters that are left out.

Written Practice

A. Write a contraction for the two underlined words.

1. I <u>will</u> help you with this job.
2. <u>We are</u> a good clean-up team.
3. <u>We have</u> the whole garage to clean.
4. <u>It is</u> such a big job.
5. <u>They have</u> made such a mess.
6. <u>She has</u> left her toys in a heap!
7. <u>He will</u> never remember to clean up.
8. <u>You are</u> such a hard worker.
9. <u>I am</u> going to take a shower when we finish.

B. Read this paragraph. Write all the contractions. Then write *P* after each one that includes a pronoun.

    Becky and Andy are in the band. Andy plays the tuba. He's practiced for many days. Becky doesn't practice with him. She'll practice her flute. She doesn't like to play with Andy. He'll play a solo. You haven't heard the band play? I wouldn't miss it for anything. It's a great band.

- **Writing Sentences**   Write five sentences to describe this picture. Use a contraction in each.

gave, given, ate, eaten

Look at the underlined words in these sentences.

I <u>gave</u> Ricardo an apple for dessert. Maria <u>has given</u> Niky an orange. We <u>have given</u> fruit to our friends. Ricardo <u>ate</u> the apple. Niky <u>has eaten</u> the orange. They <u>have eaten</u> the fruit.

Given and *eaten* always need the helping word *has* or *have*. *Gave* and *ate* do not need helping words.

> Use the helping word *has* or *have* with *given* and *eaten*.
> Do not use a helping word with *gave* and *ate*.

Practice

Choose the correct word to complete each sentence.

1. Sherry (gave, given) Tommy a present.
2. She has (gave, given) him a skateboard.
3. Tommy (gave, given) me a turn on it.
4. When we finished, we (ate, eaten) lunch.
5. We (ate, eaten) at Sherry's house.
6. We have (ate, eaten) there before.
7. Sherry's mother has (gave, given) us soup.

• **Writing Sentences** Write a sentence using *gave*. Then write one with *given*, with *ate*, and with *eaten*.

Sound Words

What word could describe the sound of a bee? Did you think of the word *buzz*?

What word would you use to describe the sound of a screen door slamming shut? Did you think of *bang*?

There are many words in our language that describe sound. Look at the words below. What might make each of these sounds?

growl   splash   screech   thump
drip   rip   boom   purr

Practice

Choose a sound word that describes each group of words below.

1. a car horn
2. a balloon breaking
3. walking up old stairs
4. an owl in the night
5. rain falling
6. glass breaking

- **Writing Sentences**   Write five words that describe sound. Then choose a sound word you can draw. Look at this drawing of *rip*. It makes the word look ripped.

Review

● **What Are Pronouns?** *(pp. 115–117)*   Write each sentence. Change the underlined word or words to a pronoun. Use these pronouns to help you: *I, you, he, she, it, we,* and *they.* One is done for you.

1. Pete sings a song.
   He sings a song.
2. Vicky is the piano player.
3. Connie plays the trumpet.
4. The trumpet is loud.
5. Jay sings too.
6. The musicians bow.
7. The music is over.
8. The people clap.
9. Jay and Pete smile.

● **More Pronouns** *(pp. 118–119)*   Write the sentence, using a pronoun in place of the underlined word or words. Use these pronouns to help you: *me, you, him, her, it, us,* and *them.*

10. Did you go to the pet store with Jud and Nan?
11. I like to pet the collie.
12. The pet store owner feeds the cats and fish.
13. He gave Lori a tiny kitten to hold.
14. He gave Nathan a spotted rabbit to pet.
15. We always enjoy playing with the animals.
16. Lori wanted to keep the kitten.
17. We all felt sad to leave the pet store.

● ***I* and *me*** *(pp. 120–121)*   Write the sentence using *I* or *me* in the blank.

18. ___ like to read about dinosaurs.
19. The car is behind ___.

20. Ernest and ____ are tennis partners.
21. Virginia sits in front of ____.
22. Perry is going with Shirley and ____.

- **Contractions** *(pp. 122–123)* Write a contraction for each pair of words. Then write a sentence for each contraction.

  23. I will   **27.** they have
  24. we are   **28.** he will
  25. you will   **29.** it is
  26. I have   **30.** she has

- **Using Words Correctly** *(p. 124)* Write the correct word that completes each sentence.

  31. The sleepy campers (ate, eaten) an early breakfast.
  32. The cook (gave, given) them scrambled eggs.
  33. The campers have (ate, eaten) scrambled eggs every day.
  34. When the campers (ate, eaten) the eggs, they frowned.
  35. Jerry (ate, eaten) his eggs very slowly.
  36. Lucy has (gave, given) her eggs to Patty.
  37. Tommy has (gave, given) his eggs to Patty.
  38. Patty (ate, eaten) all the eggs.

- **Building Vocabulary** *(p. 125)* Write a word that describes sound to complete each sentence.

  39. We heard the rain ____ on the windows.
  40. The owl ____ softly in the pine tree.
  41. The bumblebee ____ as it landed on the rose.
  42. The truck's horn ____ at the passing car.
  43. The hall floor ____ each time I stepped on it.
  44. The spilled juice ____ on the floor.

Maintain

- **Verbs** *(pp. 81–87)* Write each sentence. Use the correct verb.

  1. Meg (watches, watch) the harbor.
  2. A seagull (fly, flies) over the blue water.
  3. A white ship (sail, sails) toward the shore.
  4. Meg's father (is, am) on the ship.

  In each sentence you just wrote, put a line between the subject and the predicate. Draw a line under the verb.

- **Verbs in the Past** *(pp. 88–93)* Write each verb in past time.

5. finish	**7.** rake	**9.** fix	**11.** spy
6. clean	**8.** carry	**10.** are	**12.** scare

- **Contractions with *not*** *(pp. 94–95)* Write the contraction for each pair of words.

13. were not	**15.** have not	**17.** will not
14. do not	**16.** could not	**18.** are not

- **Pronouns** *(pp. 115–119)* Change the underlined word or words to a pronoun. Write the new sentence. Write *S* above the pronoun if it is singular. Write *P* above it if it is plural.

  19. Linda and Craig went to Disneyland.
  20. They went with Aunt Gertrude and Uncle Leroy.
  21. Aunt Gertrude drove the car.
  22. Craig toured Disneyland with Linda.

- **_I_ and _me_** _(pp. 120–121)_   Write the correct word to complete each sentence.

23. Are you going to help (I, me)?
24. (I, Me) need help with the firewood.
25. Truman and (I, me) will bring the wood indoors.
26. Father will show Truman and (I, me) how to build the fire.

- **Contractions** _(pp. 122–123)_   Write the contraction for each pair of words.

27. he is
28. we are
29. it is
30. you will
31. they are
32. it will
33. you are
34. I am

- **Using Words Correctly** _(pp. 96–97, 124)_   Write the correct word to complete each sentence.

35. Will you (came, come) to the party?
36. I remember that you (came, come) last time.
37. The dog (run, ran) to meet the mail carrier.
38. Why do dogs often (ran, run) after cats?
39. Ted (gave, given) us a scare.
40. He (eaten, ate) something bad.
41. It had (gave, given) him stomach pains.
42. The doctor asked what Ted had (ate, eaten).

- **Building Vocabulary** _(pp. 98–99, 125)_   Write the word from the box that matches each meaning.

43. the sound of paper tearing
44. a person who paints
45. not heard
46. run again
47. without speech
48. the sound of a drum

bang
rerun
speechless
rip
unheard
painter

Writing About Yourself

1 | Writing a Good Beginning

Read these two story beginnings. Which one makes you want to keep on reading?

One night we looked out the window. We were sitting and waiting for my brother.

The night was pitch dark. Aunt Donna, Kerrie, and I sat in front of the window. Where on earth could Colin be?

The first beginning does not catch your attention because it is dull. The second beginning is better. It uses exact words. It makes you want to find out what is happening.

In any story you write, your beginning sentences have to catch a reader's attention. If your beginning is good, your readers will want to keep on reading. If it is dull, they might not care what happens next in the story.

Practice

This story needs a beginning. Read this part of the story. Then write a good beginning of one or two sentences.

... Petunia didn't come home that night. I went to bed worried. Four days went by with no sign of my cat. Then on Friday afternoon, I heard a meow come from our shed. I looked inside. There was Petunia in a box with five tiny kittens.

2 | Telling Enough

Read these two paragraphs. Which one gives a clearer picture of what happened?

> We were playing the Sox. It was almost over. My team had two outs. I hit the ball far. We won.

> The Cubs were playing the Sox. It was the last inning. My team had two outs. Jamie was the runner on first. I smacked the ball into right field. It was a home run! The Cubs won by two runs.

The first paragraph does not tell exactly what happened. Some of the details are missing. The second paragraph gives more information, so you know what happened.

Every time you write, your words and sentences make a picture. That is why telling enough is so important. If you add enough details and information, your readers will have a better idea of what happened.

Practice

Read this paragraph. Do you think it tells enough?

> Dad took us to the park. We had a great time. Then we went home.

Who went with Dad? What did they do? How long did they stay? When did they leave?

Rewrite the paragraph. Change words or add new words. Give more information about what happened. Make up details so that the paragraph tells enough.

3 | Writing a Good Title

Think of the titles of your favorite books. Do they give a hint about the story? Do they make you want to read the story? Do they have just enough words so that they are easy to remember? A good title does all this.
Read the two titles and the story below.

> The Day I Woke Up and Forgot It Was Saturday
> A Mixed-up Morning

> I woke up and looked at my clock. It was 8:15! I was going to be late for school. I jumped out of bed. I put on my clothes and brushed my hair. Then I stopped short. Today was Saturday.

The first title tells too much. The second title is short and interesting. It gives just a hint about the story. Look at how capital letters are used in a title. The first word and each important word begins with a capital letter.

Practice

Write a title for the story below. Remember, a good title should make you want to read the story. Begin the first word and each important word with a capital letter.

> We waited for two hours for Dad to come home. Tonight we would get our new puppy. Then the doorbell rang. We rushed to the door. There was Dad holding a tiny puppy. Dad gave it to me to hold. It licked my face. Then it fell asleep in my arms.

4 | Getting Started

What has happened to you that you have enjoyed telling people about?

Was it something you taught your pet to do?
Was it a trip you took?
Was it something that happened on the way to school?

If you enjoy telling stories about yourself, you may also enjoy writing them. When you write a story instead of telling it, you have the chance to record what happened so you and others can enjoy it later.

Practice

Think of something special that you have done. Draw a picture of yourself to show what happened. Then show your drawing to a classmate. Tell the story that goes with the picture.

Steps for Writing About Yourself   Here are the steps for writing a story about yourself. You will follow these steps to write your own story.

Step One   Choose a topic.
Step Two   Write your story.
Step Three   Revise your story.
Step Four   Proofread your story.
Step Five   Make a final copy to share.

5 | Step One
Choose a Topic

Think about some things you have done. Ask yourself which ones would make a good story. Once you have some good ideas, you can choose the best one.

Eric thought about his special times. Then he made a list. He thought these would make good stories.

my cold drink stand
fishing last weekend at my uncle's farm
my summer at Grandma's

Eric thought about his topics. He had enjoyed selling cold drinks on a hot summer day, but it was a long time ago. Fishing last weekend had been a lot of fun. He remembered all about that. He could remember his summer at Grandma's, too, but that would be too much to write about. Finally, Eric decided that he would write about fishing with his uncle.

Assignment
- **Make a List**
- **Choose a Topic**

A. Make a list of three or four things you have done that you think would make a good story. Then ask yourself these questions.

    1. Is this about one thing that happened?
    2. Do I remember exactly what happened?
    3. Would I enjoy writing about this topic?

B. Circle the topic you think is best.

6 | Step Two
Write Your Story

Once you have chosen your topic, you are ready to write the first draft of your story. Remember to write about one thing that happened. Do not try to write about a whole summer, a whole week, or even a whole day.

As you write your first draft, get all your ideas down on paper. Remember to tell enough so that your readers will have a clear picture of what happened. Do not worry about mistakes at this point.

Eric did not worry about making mistakes in his first draft. He wanted to get his ideas in writing. He knew he would have time to correct his story later.

Eric's first draft

the Big Fish I Caught at the Farm

My uncle lives on a farm. There ~~are~~ is a lot to do there. He knows a speshul spot for fishing. We took our rods to the stream and baited our hooks. I threw out my line, and all of a sudden I felt a tug ~~and~~ my uncle said to hold on. We pulled in the biggest fish I ever saw. Uncle Joe said he didn't have a pan big enough for that whopper

Look again at Eric's first draft.

- What special time did Eric write about?
- Does Eric's title give just a hint, or does it tell too much?
- Does Eric's beginning catch your attention? Do you think he could write a better beginning?
- What interesting things did Eric tell in his story?
- What sentences give a clear picture of what happened?
- Do you have a clear picture of how the fish looked?

Now you are ready to write *your* story about yourself. Think about what would make your story interesting to a reader. Try to give a clear picture of what happened.

Assignment • Write Your First Draft

Write the first draft of your story. Remember, your first draft is just a start. Remember, too, that you will have time later on to make it better and correct any mistakes. You might want to skip a line and write on every other line. Then you will have room to make changes.

Keep these things in mind as you write.

1. Write about one thing you have done.
2. Write a good beginning that will catch a reader's attention.
3. Tell enough about what happened to give a clear picture. Use exact words.
4. Write a good title for your story. Begin the first word and each important word with a capital letter.

7 | Step Three
Revise Your Story

Eric read his story over. He decided his beginning was dull. He knew he could write a better one.

Eric also read his story to a classmate, Peter. He thought the title was too long. He and Eric thought about short, catchy titles. Peter also said that he could not picture how the fish really looked. Eric decided to make some changes in his first draft. He wrote a new title and a new beginning. He tried to give a clearer picture of the fish.

Eric's revised story

Whopper

the ~~Big Fish I Caught at the Farm~~

Last saturday Uncle Joe and I went fishing for our dinner.

My uncle lives on a farm. There ~~are~~ is a lot to

on his farm.

~~do there.~~ He knows a speshul spot for fishing.

We took our rods to the stream and baited our

hooks. I threw out my line, and all of a sudden

I felt a tug ~~and~~ my uncle said to hold on. We

a huge rainbow trout. It was a foot long.

pulled in the biggest fish ~~I ever saw~~. Uncle

Joe said he didn't have a pan big enough for

that whopper

Look carefully at Eric's revision as you answer these questions.

- How did Eric make his title better?
- Which sentences did Eric cross out at the beginning of his story? Why is his new beginning better?
- What words did Eric add to the sentence about the special spot?
- What words did he add to take the place of *the biggest fish I ever saw*?

Now you are ready to revise your story. Read it again. This time, pretend it was written by someone else. Then you will be able to look at it in a new way.

Assignment

- **Revise Your Story**
- **Discuss Your Story**

A. As you read your story again, ask yourself these questions.

1. Did I tell about one thing that happened?
2. Did I tell enough to give a clear picture?
3. Is the beginning interesting? Will my readers want to keep reading to find out more?
4. Does my title give just a hint about the story, without telling too much?

B. Make changes in your story to make it better.
C. Read your story to a classmate or your teacher. Discuss your story. Your listener may make helpful suggestions. If you think the suggestions are good, make those changes in your story.

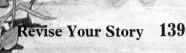

8 | Step Four
Proofread Your Story

Now you are ready to proofread and make corrections. As you proofread, check things like spelling, capital letters, end marks, and sentences.

Eric thought that his first draft was too hard to read. He decided to copy it over. Then he proofread his story.

Eric's story after proofreading

T
/the Whopper

S
Last ,saturday Uncle Joe and I went fishing for
our dinner. He knows a ~~speshul~~ spot for
             special
fishing on his farm. We took our rods to the
stream and baited our hooks. I threw out my
line, and all of a sudden I felt a tug. my uncle
                     M
said to hold on. We pulled in a huge rainbow
trout. It was a foot long. Uncle Joe said he
didn't have a pan big enough for that whopper!

- Which words did Eric correct for capital letters?
- Which word did he correct for spelling?
- Which sentences had run together? How did Eric fix them?

Practice

Proofread these sentences. There are two mistakes in each sentence. Write each sentence correctly. If you are not sure how to spell a word, look it up.

1. i could hardly wate for the big race!
2. would I win
3. I have practised hard

Assignment ● Proofread Your Story

Proofread your story. Ask yourself these questions.

1. Have I written my title correctly?
2. Is each paragraph indented?
3. Did I spell all of my words correctly?

Grammar skills checklist

4. Does each sentence tell a complete thought?
5. Does each sentence begin with a capital letter and end with the right mark?
6. Have I used helping words correctly?
7. Did I use a capital letter for the pronoun *I*?

9 | Step Five
Make a Final Copy

Eric copied his story in his best handwriting on a clean sheet of paper. He checked carefully to be sure he had copied it correctly. Now he wanted to share it with his class.

He thought about framing his story on a piece of colorful paper. Then he had an even better idea—he would make a booklet.

First, Eric got two sheets of plain paper the same size as the story paper. One sheet was for the front cover, and one was for the back cover. On the cover sheet, Eric drew a picture of himself proudly holding up a big rainbow trout. He left enough space to print the story title and his name.

Next, Eric colored in the picture carefully. Then, in large letters, he printed the title of the story. At the bottom of the cover, he wrote *by* and his own name. When the cover was finished, he placed it over his story. He placed the other sheet of paper at the back of his story. He held the papers together as his teacher stapled the left-hand edge. Now Eric's booklet was ready to read.

You have worked hard to make your story about yourself interesting and fun to read. You have also worked hard to make it correct. Now it is time to copy your story in your best handwriting on a clean sheet of paper. Once your story is finished, you should check it one more time. Make sure you have copied it correctly before you share it with your class.

Maybe you would like to do the same thing Eric did with his story—make your own special booklet.

Assignment
- **Make a Final Copy**
- **Share Your Story**

A. Write a final copy of your story in your best handwriting. Use a clean sheet of paper.

B. Check your story to make sure you have copied it without any mistakes.

C. Think of a special way to share your story.

- You can draw or paint a picture to go with the story.
- You can make a cartoon strip, with three or four frames, showing what happened in the right order.
- You can do the same thing Eric did, and make a booklet with a front and a back cover.

Mid-Book Test

- **Sentences**   Write another sentence by changing the word order. Then write if the new sentence is a *statement, question,* or *exclamation.*

   1. Room 10 played ball with our class.
   2. Did Joan hit the ball to Bill?
   3. Bill threw the ball to the shortstop.
   4. Jackie zooms past the ball!
   5. Our class beat Room 10!

- **Subjects and Predicates**   Write each sentence. Put a line between the subject and the predicate.

   6. A tornado is a big wind storm.
   7. The strong wind blows buildings and trees.
   8. Sirens warn people of the tornado.
   9. Tornadoes destroy many things.

- **Separating Sentences**   Separate each group of sentences below. Begin each sentence with a capital letter. End each sentence with the correct mark.

   10. Earl lives in the city he likes the tall buildings
   11. He rides the subway to school the ride is short
   12. The subway goes underground it moves quickly

- **Common and Proper Nouns**   Write the paragraph. Underline the nouns. Put a *C* above the common nouns. Put a *P* above the proper nouns.

   Kathy's birthday is in November. This year Kathy's birthday is on Tuesday. Kathy's mother is Mrs. Howard. Her birthday is in August. Mr. Howard's birthday is on Friday, September 3.

- **Singular and Plural Nouns**   Change the singular nouns to plural nouns. Change the plural nouns to singular nouns.

13. goose	**16.** child	**19.** feet	**22.** tooth
14. boxes	**17.** bunch	**20.** light	**23.** men
15. baby	**18.** chairs	**21.** mouse	**24.** bunnies

- **Nouns That Show Ownership**   Change the underlined words to a noun that shows ownership.

25. father of Steve	**28.** hats of the girls
26. cage of the animal	**29.** tail of the mouse
27. friends of the family	**30.** barn of the cows

- **Abbreviations**   Write the abbreviation of each word below.

31. November **32.** August **33.** Friday **34.** Monday

- **Verbs**   Write each sentence. Put a line between the subject and the predicate. Put a line under the verb.

35. We helped Dad with the logs.
36. Dad put a big log into the fireplace.
37. The fire warmed us.

- **Verbs in the Present**   Write the present time verb in ( ) that correctly completes each sentence.

38. The wind (move, moves) the sailboat.
39. The sailors (raise, raises) the sails.
40. The sails (wave, waves) in the wind.
41. The water (glisten, glistens) in the sunlight.

- **Verbs in the Past** Write the sentence, using the past time of the verb in ( ).

42. Bernie ____ to make puppets. (like)
43. He ____ an old stocking to make the puppet. (use)
44. Bernie ____ buttons for eyes. (sew)
45. He ____ to make a nose from cotton balls. (try)

- **Special Verbs** Write the past time of each underlined verb. The spelling will change.

46. Andy is on a fishing trip.
47. There are many fish.
48. The fish are very large.
49. I am happy for Andy.

- **Contractions with *not*** Write the contraction for each pair of words.

50. was not   52. cannot   54. were not
51. do not   53. did not   55. should not

- **Pronouns** Write a pronoun to replace the underlined word or words in each sentence. Write *S* if the pronoun is in the subject. Write *P* if it is in the predicate.

56. Walter and I picked up seashells.
57. The shells were on the wet sand.
58. We showed the shells to Becky.
59. Becky liked one shell very much.

- ***I* and *me*** Write the pronoun in ( ) that correctly completes each sentence.

60. Ann and (I, me) helped Jerry wash the car.
61. Jerry gave Ann and (I, me) sponges.
62. Ann and (I, me) filled a bucket with water.

- **Contractions** Write a contraction for each pair of words.

  63. she has   **66.** I am   **69.** I have
  64. you will   **67.** it is   **70.** he is
  65. they have   **68.** they will   **71.** it has

- **Using Words Correctly** Write the word in ( ) that correctly completes each sentence.

  72. Wanda has (written, wrote) a shopping list.
  73. Lorie and Wanda (gone, went) to the store together.
  74. They (did, done) their shopping quickly.
  75. Now they have (ran, run) home.
  76. They have (came, come) home too late to cook.
  77. Mother and Dad have already (ate, eaten) dinner.
  78. Mother (gave, given) them something to eat.

- **Prefixes, Suffixes, and Compounds** Write the sentences. Underline words that have prefixes or suffixes. Circle any compound words.

  79. George was the best singer in the group.
  80. The shoelace was untied.
  81. I will retie the lace.
  82. The swimmer was helpless in the deep water.
  83. Rose unwrapped the package.

- **Using Word Clues** Write the meaning of the underlined word by using clues in the sentence.

  84. The doll house had tiny furniture. There were even miniature dishes.
       a. paper   **b.** small
  85. Joe did not get to school until after ten o'clock. The teacher asked why he was tardy.
       a. late   **b.** dirty

Study Skills

1 | Using a Dictionary

Do you know how to find out the meaning of a word you do not know? If the other words in a sentence cannot help you, you should look in a dictionary. A **dictionary** is a book of words and their meanings.

The words in a dictionary are in **alphabetical order**. They are listed by the letters they begin with. Would you find *juggle* before or after *kangaroo*? The letter *j* comes before *k*. You would find *juggle* on a page before *kangaroo*.

When two words begin with the same letter, you use the second letter of each word to figure out the alphabetical order. Suppose you are looking for the word *popular*. You open the dictionary to a page on which you see the word *panel*. Is *popular* before or after *panel* in the dictionary? The word *popular* is after the word *panel* because the letter *o* comes after the letter *a*.

Practice

A. Write these words in alphabetical order.

1. mist	**4.** errand	**7.** thong
2. hoax	**5.** lotion	**8.** fern
3. spare	**6.** quick	**9.** nibble

B. These words all begin with the same letter. Write them in alphabetical order.

street	seesaw	soldier
scamper	spine	salve
sweep	shake	smolder
snow	skate	slip

2 | Finding Words in a Dictionary

The words listed in a dictionary appear in heavy, dark letters. These words are called **entry words**. Look at the dictionary sample below. What are the entry words?

made of a heavy frame with rows of metal teeth or disks. A harrow is used to break up and level off plowed ground.

harsh |härsh| —*adjective* **harsher, harshest** **1.** Rough and unpleasant: *a cold, harsh wind; a harsh voice.* **2.** Severe; stern: *The teacher seemed harsh, but he really wanted us to do well.* **3.** Cruel; unkind: *Weak animals meet with a harsh fate.*

Hart·ford |härt′fərd| The capital of Connecticut.

har·vest |här′vĭst| —*noun, plural* **harvests** **1.** The act or process of gathering in a crop: *The wheat was grown and ready for harvest in October.* **2.** The crop that is gathered: *It took a week to bring in the harvest.*
—*verb* **harvested, harvesting** To gather in: *We harvested a bumper crop of apples.*

haugh·ty |hô′tē| —*adjective* **haughtier, haughtiest** Too proud of oneself; superior in one's own mind; arrogant: *That haughty lady only speaks to rich people from old families.*

haul |hôl| —*verb* **hauled, hauling** **1.** To pull or drag with force: *It took all four of us to haul the wood to the shed.* **2.** To transport; carry; cart: *They hauled away the trash in a huge truck.*

If you wanted to find the meaning of *harvests*, would you look for the word *harvests* or the word *harvest*? You would look for *harvest*. Entry words usually are listed in simple forms, without endings such as *-ing* and *-s*. Under what entry word would you find *hauled*?

Guide words at the top of each dictionary page help you find entry words. They *guide* you to the page you need. On the dictionary sample, what are the guide words? The guide word **harsh** is the first entry word on the page. The second guide word, **haul**, is the last entry word on the page.

Every entry word on the page comes between the two guide words in alphabetical order. All the words on the sample page begin with the letters *ha*. You must look at the third or fourth letter of each word to figure the alphabetical order.

When you look up a word, find the guide words that are closest to the word you want to find. If you want to find the word *hasty*, would you look on the sample page? Would you look for the word *hawk* on that same page?

Practice

A. Use the sample page to answer these questions.

   1. What are the guide words?
   2. What is the third entry word on the page?

B. Here is a list of entry words. Write the three words that you would find on a page with the guide words **harsh/haul.**

Hawaii	hatch	hay	haste
hardware	hassock	harbor	harness

C. Write the four words that you would find on a page with the guide words **rein/relay.**

regret	report	rehearse	reject
relax	reign	relate	relative
rebel	record	remain	really

3 | Choosing the Right Definition

A dictionary tells you the meanings, or definitions, of words. A **definition** is a short sentence or a group of words. In the dictionary sample below, the definition of **cottontail** is "an American rabbit with a short, fluffy, white tail."

If there is more than one definition for a word, the definitions are numbered. The entry word **cotton** has three definitions. Often the most common meaning is listed first. Read all the definitions to be sure that you have found the meaning you need. Read the three definitions listed for **cotton**. In the dictionary sample, which meaning goes with the picture of cotton?

cot·ton |kŏt′n| —*noun* **1.** A plant that has seeds covered with soft, fluffy white fibers. Cotton is grown in warm places. **2.** The soft, fine fibers of this plant. They are used to make thread or cloth. **3.** Cloth or thread made from these fibers.

cotton gin A machine that separates cotton fibers from the seeds.

cot·ton·mouth |kŏt′n mouth′| —*noun, plural* **cottonmouths** |kŏt′n mouths′| or |kŏt′n mou*th*z| A poisonous snake. Another name for this snake is **water moccasin.**

cot·ton·tail |kŏt′n tāl| —*noun, plural* **cottontails** An American rabbit with a short, fluffy white tail.

cot·ton·wood |kŏt′n wŏod′| —*noun, plural* **cottonwoods** A tree that has seeds with white tufts that look like cotton.

couch |kouch| —*noun, plural* **couches** A piece of furniture, usually upholstered and having a back, for seating two or more persons; sofa.

cou·gar |kōō′gər| —*noun, plural* **cougars** A large wild cat. Another name for this animal is **mountain lion.**

coun·sel |koun′səl| —*noun, plural* **counsels** **1.** Advice; guidance: *Thank you for your counsel when I was in trouble.* **2.** A lawyer or group of lawyers: *the counsel for the defense.*
—*verb* **counseled, counseling** To give advice: *We counseled him to refuse the offer.*

> **coun·sel·or** |koun′sə lər| or |koun′slər| —*noun, plural*
> **counselors 1.** A person who advises or guides; adviser: *My teacher is a school counselor.* **2.** A lawyer. **3.** A person who supervises children at a summer camp.

Often a single word tells the meaning. This word is a synonym. A **synonym** has almost the same meaning as the entry word. Look at the first definition for **counsel:** What two synonyms are listed?

Sometimes the definition is followed by an example sentence or group of words. The example helps you to understand the word better. The following example sentence comes after the definition for **counsel:** *Thank you for your counsel when I was in trouble.*

Practice

A. Find each of these entry words in the sample. On your paper, write the word and the definition you find.

   1. cottonwood   **2.** couch   **3.** cotton gin

B. Write another name for each of these words.

   4. cougar   **5.** cottonmouth

C. On the sample page, find the different meanings for the word **counselor.** For each sentence below, write the number of the definition that goes with the underlined word.

   6. Wendy was a <u>counselor</u> at Camp Evergreen.
   7. Bob James went to law school to become a <u>counselor</u>.
   8. I like to talk to the <u>counselor</u> at my school.

Choosing the Right Definition   **153**

4 | Using the Library

If you wanted a book about an adventure in space, where would you find it? If you wanted to learn about dinosaurs, where would you get the facts? If you needed a book of maps, where would you go? To the library!

Libraries are full of all kinds of books. They are arranged so that you can easily find the books you want. There are places for fiction books, nonfiction books, and reference books.

The stories in **fiction books** are made up by the authors. They are not true. When you want to find a fiction book, you need to know the author's name. The books are arranged in alphabetical order by the last names of the authors. *The Mouse and the Motorcycle* is a fiction book written by Beverly Cleary. Would that book be on a shelf marked with a *C* or *M*?

Nonfiction books contain facts. They tell about real people, animals, places, and events. They are grouped by subject. For example, all the books about Africa are together. All the books about machines are together.

Do you know where you can find dictionaries and encyclopedias in your school library? They are usually with other reference books. **Reference books** are books you can use when you need special information.

If you have trouble finding something in a library, you can ask the librarian to help you. The librarian will also check out the books you want to take home.

Practice

A. Write each book title below. Next to the title write the part of the library where you would find the book. Write *fiction*, *nonfiction*, or *reference*.

1. *Winnie-the-Pooh*, by A.A. Milne, is about a bear and his friends.
2. The *World Book Encyclopedia* contains facts about many subjects.
3. *First Book of Science Experiments*, by Rose Wyler, tells how you can do experiments.
4. *Pippi Longstocking*, by Astrid Lingren, is about a girl's adventures.
5. *Maps of North America* has maps of many places.
6. *Beginning Dictionary* is for students.
7. *Blueberries for Sal*, by Robert McCloskey, tells about Sal's exciting summer.
8. *Rabbits: All About Them*, by Alvin and Virginia Silverstein, gives facts about rabbits.
9. *Turkeys, Pilgrims, and Indian Corn*, by Edna Barth, tells the history of Thanksgiving.
10. *The Riddle Monster*, by Lisl Weil, is about a prince who meets a horrible monster.

B. Beside each fiction title you wrote, now write the word you would look for to find the book.

5 | Using a Table of Contents

The **table of contents** of a book tells you what is in the book. It comes at the front, after the page that tells the title, or name, of the book. The table of contents is a list of the different chapters, or parts of the book. It tells the numbers of the pages on which the chapters begin.

The table of contents in a nonfiction book tells you what kinds of information are in the book. The titles of the chapters tell the main subjects, or main topics.

Look at the table of contents below. This table of contents is from a nonfiction book, *The Friendly Dolphins*, written by Patricia Lauber.

Read the table of contents. Would you like to read this book? You may want to read only part of a nonfiction book. *The Friendly Dolphins* has several chapters. What chapters might tell you how dolphins use sonar to locate things? You would read Chapter 6, "Dolphin Sonar." On what page does it begin?

Notice that there is an index at the end of *The Friendly Dolphins*. The next lesson will tell you about the index.

Contents

Practice

Use the table of contents to answer the questions.

1. How many chapters does *The Friendly Dolphins* have?
2. What is the title of the first chapter?
3. On what page does the chapter on baby dolphins begin?
4. To learn how dolphins play, on what page would you begin reading?
5. Which chapter will tell you about mammals in the sea?
6. On what page does the chapter on dolphin life begin?

6 | Using an Index

Often you will find an **index** in a nonfiction book. The index helps you find information. It is always at the back of the book. An index lists all the subjects, or topics, in alphabetical order. The numbers next to each subject tell you on what page or pages you can find facts about that subject. An index is longer than a table of contents.

Here is part of the index from the book *The Friendly Dolphins*. If you want to read about the pilot whale, first check the index. You will find *pilot whale* listed in the second column of the index. To get the facts about this kind of whale, you would read page 23. On what page would you find facts about the killer whale?

If a topic is discussed in several pages in a row, there is a dash between the page numbers in the index. Look at the listing for *eating: 45–47*. Eating is discussed on pages 45, 46, and 47.

Sometimes a topic is discussed in more than one part of a book. If you want to learn how dolphins play, you would read pages 10 and 11 *and* pages 50 through 56.

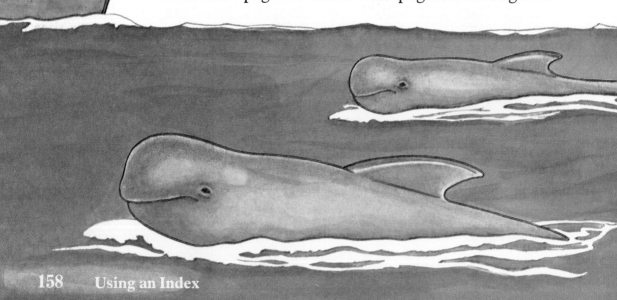

INDEX

adaptation, 36–37	friendship among
animal intelligence, 55	dolphins, 41, 58
baleen, 17–18	games, 51–56
bats, 67	hydrophone, 64, 65
birth, 40–42	
blubber, 34–37	intelligence, 50–61
blue whale, 19	killer whale, 19
breathing, 16, 17, 32, 44	mammals, 16, 36, 40
cold-blooded animals, 34	Marineland, 50–52, 69
eating, 45–47	pilot whale, 23
echo-location, 67–75	play, 10–11, 50–56
emotions, 57–58	porpoises, 16, 18, 19
flippers, 26, 27, 31	problem-solving, 56, 57

Practice

A. Write the answers to these questions.

1. Where is the index located in a book?
2. In *The Friendly Dolphins*, on what page can you find facts about bats?
3. On what pages can you read about friendship among dolphins?
4. On what pages can you read about baleen?

B. Write the following topics on your paper. Then write *yes* if the topic is listed in the index. Write *no* if it is not in the index.

5. Marineland	7. blubber	9. play
6. gills	8. echo-location	10. reptiles

Writing a Report

1 | Telling Facts

There are some things that everyone knows to be true. These things are called **facts.** The sentences below tell facts.

> Giraffes have long necks.
> There are many colors of crayons.

Some sentences tell what people think or feel. Not all people think or feel the same way. The sentences below tell what some people think or feel.

> Green apples taste good.
> Playing baseball is fun.

These sentences do not tell facts. Some people may not like the taste of green apples. Not all people enjoy playing baseball.

Practice

Read the sentences below. Number your paper for each sentence. Circle the numbers of the sentences that tell facts.

1. Dogs have four legs.
2. A dog is an animal.
3. A dog makes the best pet.
4. Baby dogs are called puppies.
5. Puppies are more fun than kittens.
6. A poodle is a kind of dog.
7. Big dogs are nicer than little dogs.
8. Dogs can wag their tails.

2 | Keeping to the Main Idea

The main idea is what a paragraph is about. The topic sentence tells the main idea of a paragraph. The topic sentence is often the first sentence in the paragraph. The other sentences in the paragraph should all tell about the main idea.

Read this paragraph. Think about the main idea. Look for the sentence that does not keep to the main idea.

> Plant parts can be used to make dyes for yarn and cloth. Bark, roots, flowers, and berries are some plant parts used to make dyes. Cherries and beets make different red colors. Brown can be made from walnuts. Walnuts taste good. Onion skins make a light yellow.

The main idea is that plant parts can be used to make dyes. The first sentence is the topic sentence. It tells the main idea.

The sentence *Walnuts taste good* does not keep to the main idea. It does not tell about making dyes.

Practice

A. Read the paragraph below. Write the topic sentence. Think about the main idea given in the topic sentence. Then write the sentence that does not keep to the main idea.

The arctic fox is able to keep warm in cold weather. It has thick, warm fur. Hair between the pads on its paws protects its feet from the cold ground. The fox is a beautiful animal. It can wrap its long tail around its body to keep warm when it sleeps.

B. Follow the directions for exercise A for the paragraph below.

Horses helped the pioneers in many ways. A horse is bigger than a pony. The horses pulled the pioneers' plows and wagons. They carried the people on their backs. They also carried heavy packs. Some horses were even their owners' best friends.

3 | Taking Notes

Sometimes you may read or hear facts or ideas that you would like to remember. A good way to remember the information is to take notes. When you take notes, you write only enough words to help you remember the main ideas and important facts.

Read the paragraph below. What is the main idea? What are the important facts?

> The flat roofs of apartment buildings are used in many ways. Some roofs have fenced playgrounds. On other roofs, people grow their own vegetable gardens in pots. Some roofs even have little parks with trees and flowers.

A good way to take notes is to write the main idea first. Then write a few words to tell the important facts. Read these notes for the paragraph about the roofs.

> Flat rooftops of apartment buildings are used in many ways.
> 1. for playgrounds
> 2. for growing vegetables in pots
> 3. for parks

The topic sentence is written above the notes. It tells the main idea. The important facts are told with just a few words.

Practice

A. Read the paragraph below. Write the topic sentence. Then write notes to help you remember the important facts.

Some American Indian tribes in the Northwest made totem poles. Tall, straight logs were used for poles. The Indians carved heads of birds and animals into the poles. Then they painted the carvings. They put the poles in front of their homes.

B. Follow the directions for exercise A to take notes on the paragraph below.

Parrots can learn to do many things. Almost all parrots can learn to talk. Some parrots can also bark and whistle. Parrots can learn tricks, such as roller skating and riding a scooter. Some parrots can even add and subtract.

4 | Getting Started

Writing a report is a good way to learn new information about a topic. You might want to learn about sharks. You might want to find out about icebergs. You can find the facts you want to know in books and encyclopedias. Your report tells the facts you learned.

A report tells only facts. It does not tell how you think or feel about the topic.

Practice

Which topics below could be report topics?

1. butterflies
2. what I like to eat
3. my favorite story
4. my best birthday
5. seashells
6. the first Thanksgiving

Steps for Writing a Report   Here are the steps for writing a report. You will follow these steps to write your own report.

Step One   Choose a topic.
Step Two   Plan your report.
Step Three Write your report.
Step Four   Revise your report.
Step Five   Proofread your report.
Step Six   Make a final copy to share.

5 | Step One
Choose a Topic

Here are two guides for choosing a good report topic.

1. Choose a topic that interests you.
2. Choose a topic that you can find facts for easily.

Justine's class was going to write reports. They decided to write about wild animals. The students named different wild animals they wanted to learn about. They named these animals.

raccoon   chipmunk   kangaroo   wolf   elephant

Each student chose one of these animals or another wild animal as a report topic. Justine chose the kangaroo. She knew that kangaroos carried their babies in pouches. She wanted to learn other facts about them.

Assignment
- **Make a List of Topics**
- **Choose a Topic**

A. With your class, make a list of report topics.
B. Choose the topic that you find most interesting.

6 | Step Two
Plan Your Report

Justine wondered what facts she should put in her report. She could not tell everything about kangaroos.

The students talked about what they most wanted to learn about the animals. They decided on two questions that they wanted their reports to answer.

1. What does the animal look like?
2. Where does it live?

Justine took two pieces of paper. At the top of one page, she wrote, "What does a kangaroo look like?" On the other, she wrote, "Where do kangaroos live?"

Then the class talked about where they could find the answers to their questions. They named two places, the encyclopedia and library books.

Justine went to the library. The librarian helped her find pages in the encyclopedia that told about kangaroos. Justine looked through the pages for facts about the way kangaroos look.

Justine took notes to help her remember the facts. She wrote her notes on the paper with the first question.

Read Justine's notes below.

> *What does a kangaroo look like?*
> 1. *about six feet tall*
> 2. *small head*
> 3. *large pointed ears*

> 4. small front legs
> 5. strong back legs
> 6. long tail helps it sit up and hop
> 7. mother has a pouch for carrying babies
> <u>Britannica Junior Encyclopedia,</u>
> Volume 9, pages 2-3

As Justine read more of the encyclopedia pages, she found the facts to answer the second question for her report. She took notes to remember those facts, too. At the bottom of her papers, she copied the title and volume number of the encyclopedia and the numbers of the pages she had used.

Assignment

- Make a List of Questions
- Find Facts
- Take Notes

A. With your class, write two questions to answer in your reports.

B. Get a clean piece of paper for each question. Write one question at the top of each page.

C. Find a book or encyclopedia page about your topic. Read for facts to answer each question you wrote.

D. Take notes to help you remember the facts.

E. Write the name and page numbers of the book or the encyclopedia you used. If you used a book, write the author's name. If you used an encyclopedia, write the volume number.

7 | Step Three
Write Your Report

You should have all the facts for your report in your notes. Before you begin, you must decide how many paragraphs your report will have. You must also decide what facts will be in each paragraph.

Justine decided to write one paragraph for each of her questions. The first paragraph would tell what kangaroos look like. The second paragraph would tell where they live.

Justine followed these steps to write each paragraph.

1. She used her question as the topic sentence.
2. She read her notes again.
3. She wrote the facts in her notes in complete sentences to make a paragraph. She wrote her sentences in an order that made sense.

Justine did not worry about mistakes as she wrote. She knew that she could correct them later.

Justine's first draft

What does a kangaroo look like? It is about six feet tall. My Dad is six feet tall. It has a small head. It has large pointed ears. It has small front legs it has big strong back legs. It has a long tail to help it sit up The mother Kangaroo has a pouch to carry her babies.

Where do kangaroos live? They live on the grasslands. ~~They also~~ some kangaroos live in trees in the forrests. I would like to go there to see them.

- What is the topic sentence of each paragraph?
- Do the sentences in each paragraph keep to the main idea? Tell any sentences that do not.
- Did Justine tell only facts in her report?

Assignment • **Write Your First Draft**

Write the first draft for your report. Write one paragraph for each question that you wrote. You may want to skip a line as you write.

Follow these steps to write each paragraph.

1. Write the question as the topic sentence for the paragraph.
2. Read your notes again. Think about the main idea of the paragraph.
3. Write the facts in your notes in complete sentences. Keep to the main idea.
4. Write only facts.

8 | Step Four
Revise Your Report

Justine read her first draft again after a few days. She saw that she did not keep to the main idea in her first paragraph. She also saw that she told some of her own feelings in the second paragraph. She crossed out those sentences.

Justine saw that she forgot to tell the country where kangaroos live. She added a sentence to her second paragraph.

Justine read her report to Jenny. Jenny pointed out that too many sentences began with the words *It has*. It made the report sound boring. Justine changed one of these sentences to make her report sound better.

Justine added a title to her report. She wrote it at the top of her paper. She also wrote the title, volume number, and page numbers of the encyclopedia she had used at the end of her report.

Read Justine's revised report on the next page.

Justine's revised report

The Kangaroo

What does a kangaroo look like? It is about six feet tall. My Dad is six feet tall. It has a small head, _and_ It has large pointed ears. It has small front legs it has big strong back legs. It has a long tail to help it sit up The mother Kangaroo has a pouch to carry her babies.

Where do kangaroos live? _Kangaroos live in australia._ They live on the grasslands. ~~They also~~ some kangaroos live in trees in the forrests. I would like to go there to see them.

Britannica Junior Encyclopedia, Volume 9, pages 2–3

- What sentences did Justine take out? Why?
- What sentence did Justine add? Why?
- What two sentences did Justine make into one sentence? Why?

Assignment
- **Revise Your Report**
- **Discuss Your Report**

A. Read your report again to yourself. Ask yourself the questions below. Make any corrections that are needed.

1. Did you write a question as the topic sentence for each paragraph? Underline the question.
2. Does every sentence in each paragraph keep to the main idea? Cross out any sentences that do not keep to the main idea.
3. Does each paragraph tell only facts? Cross out any sentences that tell what you think or feel.
4. Are your sentences boring? Add words or rewrite sentences to make them more interesting.
5. Write a title for your report.
6. Write the title of the book or encyclopedia you used to find your facts. If there is an author, write the author's name, too.

B. Read your report to a classmate or your teacher. Discuss how to make your report better. If your listener has good suggestions, or if you have thought of anything else, make the changes in your report.

9 | Step Five
Proofread Your Report

You must proofread your report before you make a final copy. Look for spelling mistakes. Be sure you used capital letters and end marks correctly. Be sure all sentences have a subject and a predicate.

Justine copied her report to make it easier to read. Then she proofread it. Look at the first paragraph from her report after she proofread it.

Justine's report after proofreading

> The Kangaroo
>
> What does a kangaroo look like? It is about six feet tall. It has a small head and large pointed ears. It has small front legs *and* ~~it~~ has strong back legs. It has a long tail to help it sit up The mother ^k^Kangaroo has a pouch to carry her babies.

- What capital letter did Justine change? Why?
- What punctuation mark did she add? Why?
- What other correction did Justine make? Why?

Practice

Proofread the second paragraph from Justine's report below. There are three mistakes. Write the paragraph correctly. Look up the spelling of any word you are not sure of in a dictionary.

Where do kangaroos live? Kangaroos live in australia. They live on the grasslands. some kangaroos live in trees in the forrests.

- What three corrections did you make? Why?

Assignment • Proofread Your Report

Proofread your report. Ask yourself these questions.

1. Are all my words spelled correctly?
2. Are my paragraphs indented?

Grammar skills checklist

3. Does each sentence tell one complete thought?
4. Does each sentence begin with a capital letter and end with the correct mark?
5. Did I use capital letters correctly?
6. Did I use pronouns correctly?

10 | Step Six
Make a Final Copy

The last step is to make a final copy of your report. The final copy will be written in your best handwriting. Other people may want to read your report.

Justine copied her report neatly. She checked it again for any mistakes.

The students in Justine's class wanted to read their reports out loud. Justine practiced reading her report at home. When she read it to the class, Justine showed pictures of kangaroos she had found in books. She also showed where Australia is on a map. She borrowed the encyclopedia in which she had found her facts. She thought some students might want to read more facts about kangaroos.

Assignment

- **Make a Final Copy**
- **Share Your Report**

A. Copy your report neatly.
B. Check your report again for any mistakes.
C. Think of a special way to share your report.

- You may want to read your report out loud as Justine did. Show books, pictures, or other materials that would help explain your topic.
- You can make a poster. Draw a picture of your report topic.

Punctuation

1 | Reviewing End Marks

Punctuation marks separate words and sentences. They help make the meaning clear. The period (.), the question mark (?), and the exclamation mark (!) are end marks. A period ends a statement. A question mark ends a question. An exclamation mark ends an exclamation.

Try It Out

End each sentence with the correct punctuation mark.

Do you like to take pictures __ I like to take color pictures __ Is there film in the camera __ I'll take a picture of you __ What a great hobby this is __

> The period (.), the question mark (?), and the exclamation mark (!) are end marks.

Written Practice

Copy these sentences correctly. Begin each sentence with a capital letter. End each one with the correct mark.

Roberto Clemente was a baseball superstar __ he was born in Puerto Rico __ was Clemente a great hitter __ he was terrific __ he batted 3000 hits __

- **Writing a Paragraph** Write a story about something exciting that happened. Use three different end marks.

2 | Commas in a Series

A comma (,) is another punctuation mark. You have used commas when writing dates and addresses. Commas are also used to separate words in sentences. Read this sentence.

Betty Ann and Mike are building a snow fort.

How many children are building a snow fort? Are there two children? Are there three children?

Now read this sentence. How many children are there?

Betty, Ann, and Mike are building a snow fort.

Three children are named in this sentence. The commas separate the names. The commas help you understand the sentence.

Three or more words listed together are a **series**. Commas are used to separate words in a series.

Does this sentence list words in a series?

Teri's favorite cats are Tasha and Mittens.

This sentence lists only two things, Tasha and Mittens. Two things do not make a series. This sentence does not need commas.

Does this sentence list words in a series?

Tom's favorite cats are Fluffy, Patches, and Tiger.

Yes, three words are listed in this sentence. They are separated by commas. What are the words in the series?

Try It Out

Tell which sentences use commas correctly. If the sentence does not use commas correctly, tell how you would correct it.

1. Dennis, Jon, and Len are in my class.
2. I like math reading and spelling.
3. I bought a sandwich and fruit.
4. I had tomatoes lettuce and cheese in my sandwich.
5. I could choose a banana peach, or orange.

> ▶ A list of three or more words is a **series**. Commas separate words in a series.

Written Practice

Write each sentence. Put commas in the correct places in each series.

1. Alice Bob and Emily came over on Sunday.
2. We shopped for tomatoes celery and lettuce.
3. We also bought apples oranges and pears.
4. I took the milk butter and cheese out of the bag.
5. We had spaghetti bread and salad for dinner.
6. We read talked and played games after dinner.
7. Mom Dad and Grandma Rose played with us.
8. We watched football soccer and tennis on TV.
9. We will do this again in June July or August.

- **Writing Sentences** Write a sentence, using a series of three or more things you like to do. Then write a sentence, using three or more names in a series.

3 | Quotation Marks

You have read many stories in which people talk to each other. Punctuation marks show you what the people say. Read these sentences.

Alice asked, "Why are you hurrying?"
The rabbit said, "I'm late for an important date."

Quotation marks (" ") are punctuation marks. They set off the spoken word. Quotation marks are put at the beginning and end of the exact words someone says. What did Alice ask? What did the rabbit say? You can tell what Alice and the rabbit said because their exact words are inside quotation marks. Their exact words are called a **quotation.**

The words *Alice asked* and *The rabbit said* tell you who did the talking. Alice and the rabbit did not say those words. Those words are *not* inside the quotation marks.

Read these sentences.

Nelson said, "My grandparents live on a ranch."
Julie asked, "Where is the ranch?"

What are Nelson's and Julie's exact words? How do you know?

Try It Out

Tell where to put the quotation marks in each sentence.

1. Carmen said, Look at my terrarium!
2. Eddie asked, What is a terrarium?
3. Carmen answered, It is a garden inside a bottle.

4. Eddie asked, How did you make it?
5. Carmen said, I put some soil in the bottle and added a few small plants.
6. Eddie asked, How do the plants get water?
7. Carmen answered, I squirt water from a bottle.
8. Eddie asked, Why is the lid on the jar?
9. Carmen said, The lid keeps the soil from drying out.
10. Eddie exclaimed, Your terrarium is great!

▶ A speaker's exact words are called a **quotation.**
▶ **Quotation marks** (" ") are punctuation marks used at the beginning and end of a speaker's exact words.

Written Practice

Write each sentence. Add the quotation marks.

1. Craig said, Let's go to the library today.
2. Bill asked, Why?
3. Craig answered, The library has some new books about the old West.
4. Bill exclaimed, I love to read about the West!
5. Craig said, They have books about cattle brands.
6. Bill said, I like to read about famous people.
7. Craig asked, Who is your favorite?
8. Bill answered, Pecos Bill is my favorite.
9. Craig exclaimed, He wasn't even real!

• **Writing Sentences**   Write a talk between you and a friend. Use quotation marks correctly.

4 | More About Quotations

You have learned that quotation marks set off someone's exact words. The words that tell you who is talking are *not* put inside the quotation marks. They are not part of the quotation. Read these sentences.

> Mrs. King asked, "What bird lays the biggest eggs?"
> Willie said, "The ostrich lays the biggest eggs."
> Angie added, "An ostrich egg can weigh four pounds!"

The words *Mrs. King asked*, *Willie said*, and *Angie added* tell you who is speaking. They are separated from the speaker's exact words by a comma.

Look at the first word after each beginning quotation mark. Do these words start with capital letters? *What*, *The*, and *An* all start with capital letters. Each word is the first word of a quotation.

What punctuation mark ends Mrs. King's question? What punctuation mark ends Willie's statement? What punctuation mark ends Angie's exclamation? Are the end marks before or after the quotation marks? Put the end mark for a quotation before, or inside, the last quotation mark.

Try It Out

Read the sentences. Tell where to put commas, capital letters, and end marks. Tell which end marks to use.

1. Louetta said "let's go sled riding"
2. Kelly asked "where should we go"
3. Louetta said "let's go to Batten Park Hill"

4. Kelly answered "that's a long hill to climb"

5. Louetta exclaimed "the ride down is just as long"

> Use a comma to separate the exact quotation from the rest of the sentence. Begin the first word of a quotation with a capital letter. Put the end mark inside the last quotation mark.

Written Practice

Write each sentence. Use a comma to separate the speaker's exact words from the rest of the sentence. Put capital letters and end marks in the correct places.

1. Jon called "look at my new kite"

2. Tom asked "will it fly"

3. Patty said "i'll hold the string"

4. Jon said "i'll start running"

5. Patty shouted "you're running the wrong way"

6. Tom said "it will catch in a tree"

7. Patty said "now you're all right"

8. Jon and Tom cried "look at the kite flying"

- **Writing Sentences** Write a riddle or joke. Write it as if one person is saying it to another person. Use quotations.

5 Using Words Correctly

bring, brought

Look at the underlined words in these sentences.

I <u>bring</u> my new bike. I <u>brought</u> my new bike.
She <u>brings</u> her new bike. She <u>brought</u> her new bike.

Some verbs change their spelling when they change from present time to past time. *Bring* changes to *brought*.

Use *bring* or *brings* in the present. Use *brought* in the past.

Practice

Complete each sentence with the form of *bring* given in ( ). The first one has been done for you.

1. Each week we ____ things to class to show. (present)
   bring
2. This week Eli ____ his pet white mouse. (past)
3. Last week he ____ his pet toad. (past)
4. Each week he ____ a different pet. (present)
5. Mother says I can ____ my hamster today. (present)

● **Writing Sentences**   Write five sentences about a party. Use *bring* in three sentences and *brought* in two.

took, taken

Look at the underlined words in these sentences.

I <u>took</u> piano lessons. I <u>have taken</u> piano lessons.
He <u>took</u> piano lessons. He <u>has taken</u> piano lessons.

The sentences on the left show that *took* needs no helping word. The ones on the right use *have* or *has* with *taken*.

Use the helping word *has* or *have* with *taken*.
Took does not need a helping word.

Practice

A. Choose the correct word to complete each sentence.

My grandmother (took, taken) pictures for a living. She (took, taken) very good pictures of people. She has (took, taken) many pictures of weddings. She (took, taken) the pictures of my sister's wedding last year. She has (took, taken) pictures of my brother and me, too.

B. Complete each sentence with the correct word.

1. Our family has (took, taken) many car trips.
2. We (took, taken) a trip to the West last summer.
3. We (took, taken) many country roads on our trip.
4. I (took, taken) a picture of an old mining town.
5. My sister has (took, taken) many pictures, too.

• **Writing Sentences**   Write five sentences. Use *taken* in two sentences and *took* in the other three.

Words from Other Languages

How many languages can you use? Before you answer, try to answer these questions.

What do we call the year of school before first grade?
What do we hold above our heads to keep us dry when it rains?
What do we call a rope with a loop at the end used for catching cows?

Did you answer the questions correctly? If you did, you were speaking in other languages. The answers to these questions are words from other languages. *Kindergarten* is a German word. It means "garden of children." *Umbrella* is a word from Italy. The people of Italy used umbrellas to keep the sun off their heads. We use umbrellas to keep off rain. *Lasso* is a word that comes from the Spanish language.

The English language is made up of words from many languages. Some words come from languages of Native Americans. Other words were added from the different languages the settlers spoke.

Many words for foods come from other languages. The words come from the languages of the countries where the foods were made. *Pizza* and *spaghetti* come from Italian. The Mexicans brought the words *tortilla* and *taco* for two of their foods. *Tea* is from the Chinese language.

Names for animals come from the languages of many countries. *Chimpanzee* comes from a West African language. *Kangaroo* comes from Australia. The word *raccoon* is from a Native American language called Algonquian.

People still come to the United States from many lands. In time they too will add more words to our language.

Practice

Complete each sentence with a word from the box. Use each word once.

kindergarten	raccoon	taco
umbrella	chimpanzee	pizza
spaghetti	lasso	kangaroo

1. A food made of long, thin noodles and served with tomato sauce is called ____.
2. My favorite ____ has sausage and extra cheese on it.
3. An animal with a natural face mask is a ____.
4. A mother ____ carries her baby in her pouch.
5. A ____ is a kind of ape.
6. The year of school before first grade is called ____.
7. The cowhand caught the calf with a ____.
8. I use my ____ when it rains.
9. A kind of Mexican food is a ____.

- **Writing Sentences** Choose any five words from the box. Write a sentence for each one.

Review

- **Reviewing End Marks** *(p. 179)* Write each sentence. Use a correct punctuation mark at the end.

  1. What are masks made of
  2. They can be made of many things
  3. Masks can be made of wood or rubber
  4. Look at this scary mask
  5. It looks like a monster
  6. Would you like to make a mask

- **Commas in a Series** *(pp. 180–181)* Write each sentence. Put the commas in the correct places in the series. If the sentence does not need commas, write *correct*.

  7. Ms. Todd Mrs. Chu and Mr. Stone are salespeople.
  8. They sell clothes jewelry and shoes.
  9. Ms. Todd works on Monday and Thursday.
  10. Mrs. Chu sells shoes and boots.
  11. Mr. Stone sells rings pins and necklaces.

- **Quotation Marks** *(pp. 182–183)* Write each sentence. Put quotation marks in the correct places in each sentence.

  12. Tim asked, Can I enter the wheelchair races?
  13. Dad answered, Yes, if you want to.
  14. Tim said, I can beat Larry.
  15. Dad asked, How old is Larry?
  16. Tim said, He's three years older than I am.
  17. Dad exclaimed, You must be pretty fast!

- **More About Quotations** *(pp. 184–185)* Write each sentence. Put quotation marks, commas, capital letters, and end marks in the correct places.

  18. Lin asked would you like to go to Funland
  19. Becky exclaimed yes, I love Funland
  20. Lin said my favorite part is the Fun House
  21. Becky said the strange mirrors make me laugh
  22. Lin said i like sliding down the chute

- **Using Words Correctly** *(pp. 186–187)* Complete each sentence with the correct word.

  23. Carrie has (took, taken) tumbling lessons.
  24. She (took, taken) them last year.
  25. She (took, taken) them after school.
  26. Cora and Ellie have (took, taken) the lessons also.

  Write the form of *bring* shown in (   ).

  27. Each week Simon _____ home an animal. (present)
  28. Last week he _____ a bird with a broken wing. (past)
  29. Another week he _____ a tiny mouse. (past)
  30. I always like to see what he _____. (present)

- **Building Vocabulary** *(pp. 188–189)* Match each word with its meaning.

  31. lasso   **a.** pie crust topped with tomato sauce and cheese (Italian)
  32. kindergarten   **b.** a covering for the rain (Italian)
  33. pizza   **c.** a kind of ape (West African)
  34. chimpanzee   **d.** rope with a loop on the end (Spanish)
  35. umbrella   **e.** year of school before first grade (German)

Writing a Letter

1 | The Five Parts of a Letter

HEADING	76 South Boulevard Richmond, Virginia 23232 November 4, 1983
GREETING	Dear Aunt Kathy,
BODY	I love the gloves you knitted for my birthday. They are just the same color as my coat. Now I am going to get some red boots, too! I hope you come and visit us soon.
CLOSING	Love from your niece,
SIGNATURE	*Susan*

Look at the **heading** of the letter.

- What does it tell?
- What words begin with capital letters?
- How many commas are there? Where are they?

Find the **greeting.**

- What words begin with capital letters?
- What mark follows the greeting?

Look at the **body** of the letter. The body is made up of paragraphs. Are the paragraphs indented?
Find the **closing.** It is lined up with the heading.

- What word begins with a capital letter?
- What mark comes after the closing?

Find the **signature.** When you sign your name, you are writing your signature.

Practice

Here are five parts of a letter. They are not in order. Write them on your paper with every part in the correct place.

Your friend,

32 West Street
Ocean, New Jersey 07712
November 15, 1983

Dear Sandy,

Judy

I can hardly wait to come and see you in Florida. It's very cold here. Can we really wear our swimsuits in December?

2 | Addressing an Envelope

For your letter to be delivered quickly, your envelope needs the **address** of the person you are writing. It also needs a **return address.** The return address is the address of the person writing the letter.

Read the names of the two parts of the envelope. Look at where the two parts are placed.

RETURN
ADDRESS

Donna McCarthy
R.D. 2
Southfield, Vermont 05663

ADDRESS

Mrs. Daniel Kurtz
212 Fox Street
Pittsburgh, Pennsylvania 15213

- What words begin with capital letters?
- Where are commas placed in the addresses?

Practice

Draw an envelope on a piece of paper. Use the following address. Use your own name and address in the return address. Make sure you have used capital letters and commas correctly.

Mr. John Marshall
142 Garden Street
Goshen, Indiana 46526

3 | Getting Started

Does someone you like live far away? You may not be able to talk to each other very often, but there is another way to tell each other things. You can say, "Happy Birthday," or, "Guess what happened to me!" You can say, "Thank you," or, "I hope you feel better." You can do all these things by writing letters.

Writing letters is different from other writing you do in two ways. First, when you write a letter you are usually writing to one person only. Second, when you write a letter, you often get a letter back!

Practice

Can you think of someone you would like to write to? Get out a pencil and a piece of paper. Write down the names of some people who would like to get a letter from you. Think of as many people as you can.

Steps for Writing a Letter   Here are the steps for writing a letter. You will follow these steps to write a letter of your own.

Step One	Choose a topic.
Step Two	Write your letter.
Step Three	Revise your letter.
Step Four	Proofread your letter.
Step Five	Make a final copy of your letter and mail it.

4 | Step One
Choose a Topic

Before you write a letter to someone, think about what that person would like to hear. What would you say if you were talking to that person?

Kenji had just moved to Texas. He had a lot of friends and relatives back in California. There were four people he wanted to write to, but his grandmother was the most important. Kenji made a list of the things she might like to know.

the new school

the soccer team

the new house

Assignment

- **Make a List**
- **Choose a Topic**

A. Decide on the person you will write to. Then make a list of the things you might like to say.

B. Look at your list. Which topic would the person most like to hear about? What would you most like to write about? Decide on the topic of your letter and circle it on your list.

5 | Step Two
Write Your Letter

Kenji decided to write to his grandmother about his soccer team. He got out a piece of paper and wrote down what he wanted to say. He made some mistakes, but he did not worry about them at this point.

Kenji's first draft

> Dear Grandma,
>
> Guess what! I'm on the soccer team at school. Remember how I practised kicking with Dad. I can really kick a ball now. I think I ~~prob~~ want to be a goalie. I'm learning how to catch the ball when somebody kicks it really hard. I'm getting alot better.

- Did Kenji write about one main thing?
- What did Kenji say that shows he is talking to his grandmother and not just writing about soccer?

Remember to do these things when you write your letter.

- Think about the person you are writing to.
- Think about what that person would enjoy hearing.
- Write about one main thing.
- Try to let the person know you are really thinking of him or her.
- Use exact words to make your letter interesting.

Assignment • Write Your First Draft

Write down on a piece of paper what you want to say in your letter. This will be your first draft. If you skip a line, it will be easier to make changes later.

6 | Step Three
Revise Your Letter

Now you have written the message for your letter. You have put down what you want to say. Would you like to get a letter like the one you have written? Are there things you could do to make it better?

Kenji read over his letter. He thought of something else he wanted to say to his grandmother. He added two sentences at the end.

Then Kenji read his letter to Jerry. He wanted to make sure it was a good letter.

Jerry said, "I like your letter. I think it's good."

"Does it sound like I'm talking to my grandmother?" asked Kenji.

"I don't know," said Jerry. "All the sentences sound the same. Do they all start with *I*?"

Kenji looked back at his letter. Six of his sentences started the same way! He thanked Jerry and went back to his desk. He thought of ways to change some of his sentences so they did not all sound the same. You can see Kenji's changes below.

Kenji's revised letter

> Dear Grandma,
>
> Guess what! I'm on the soccer team at school.
>
> Remember how I practised kicking with Dad.
> My coch says
> I can really kick a ball now. I think I ~~prob~~

want to be a goalie. I'm learning how to catch the ball when somebody kicks it really hard. I'm getting alot better.

Its

easier

I miss you. Write to me soon.

- What sentences did Kenji change?
- Why did he change these sentences?
- What did he add to his letter?

Assignment • Revise Your Letter

A. Read your letter to yourself. Ask yourself these questions.

1. Does my letter sound as though I am talking to the person?
2. Is what I told about interesting? Could I add anything else?
3. Do most of my sentences start in the same way? Could I change some of them?
4. Is there anything else I would really like to say to this person?
5. Will this letter make the person feel like writing back?

B. Read your letter to someone else. Ask for ideas for making it better. If your listener has good ideas, or if you have thought of anything else, make more changes in your letter.

7 | Proofread Your Letter

Now you are ready to look over your letter to check for mistakes. This is the time to make sure you have used capital letters and punctuation marks correctly. It is the time to check the spelling of your words. This checking is called proofreading.

Kenji decided to copy his letter over before he proofread it. He added the heading and the closing. Then he checked it for errors.

Kenji's letter after proofreading

26 River *D*rive

Dallas, Texas 76013

May 22, 1983

Dear Grandma,

Guess what! I'm on the soccer team at school.

Remember how I ~~practised~~ *practiced* kicking with Dad. *?*

My ~~coch~~ *coach* says I can really kick a ball now.

I think I want to be a goalie. I'm learning how to catch the ball when somebody kicks it really hard. It's getting alot easier.

I miss you. Write to me soon.

> *Love from your grandson,*
> *Kenji*

- What spelling mistakes did Kenji correct?
- What punctuation mistakes did he correct?

Practice

This letter has nine mistakes in using capital letters and commas. There is one spelling error. Rewrite the letter, correcting the ten mistakes.

> 8 spring Street
> portland oregon 97215
> October 15 1983

dear Jan

I'm sending you to of the best cartoons I have drawn. Will you send me some of yours?

> your friend
> *Ellen*

Assignment • **Proofread Your Letter**

Before you proofread your letter, write the heading at the top. Then read over your letter, looking for mistakes. Ask yourself these questions.

1. Are my paragraphs indented?
2. Are all the words spelled correctly?
3. Have I used capital letters and commas correctly in the heading and the greeting and the closing?

Grammar skills checklist

4. Does each sentence tell a complete thought?
5. Have I corrected any sentences that run together?
6. Have I used commas and end marks correctly?

8 | Step Five
Make a Final Copy

Now you are ready to copy over your letter. You might want to use special paper for writing letters. You could also use a plain sheet of paper.

Kenji decided to make his own special paper for this letter. He took a sheet of plain paper and colored a soccer ball in the top left corner. Then he copied over his letter in his best handwriting. He read it over again to make sure he had not made any new mistakes. Down one side he drew a picture of himself playing soccer.

Then he addressed an envelope, put his letter in it, put a stamp on the envelope, and mailed it to his grandmother.

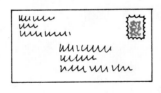

Assignment
- **Make a Final Copy**
- **Mail Your Letter**

A. Make a final copy of your letter in your best handwriting. Use special paper for letters, or make your own by drawing or painting on plain paper.

B. Check your letter to make sure you have copied it without any mistakes.

C. Address your envelope carefully, put a stamp on it, and mail your letter.

Adjectives

1 | What Is an Adjective?

Read these sentences.

> The bicycle belongs to the girl.
> The <u>red</u> bicycle belongs to the <u>little</u> girl.

The second sentence gives you details about the bicycle and the girl. It tells you the bicycle is red and the girl is little. The words *red* and *little* describe, or tell about, the nouns *bicycle* and *girl*. A word that describes a noun is called an **adjective**.

Adjectives can make sentences more interesting. They give us details. They help us *see* the people, places, and things they describe. Different adjectives can make us see, or think of, different pictures. Read these sentences.

> The <u>sad</u> clown wore a <u>flowered</u> hat.
> The <u>happy</u> clown wore a <u>pointed green</u> hat.
> The <u>silly</u> clown wore a <u>floppy brown</u> hat.
> The <u>tall</u>, <u>skinny</u> clown wore a <u>tiny</u> hat.

Each sentence tells about a clown and his or her hat. Try to picture each sentence in your mind. How do you picture the different clowns? Which words are the adjectives?

The adjectives above tell you *what* clown wore *what kind* of hat. Adjectives can also tell you *how many*. Read this sentence.

> The *three* children bought *two* bags of peanuts.

How many children bought peanuts? How many bags of peanuts did they buy? The adjectives *three* and *two* tell how many.

Try It Out

Read each sentence. Tell the adjectives. Tell the nouns they describe.

1. The brave trainer shouted at the angry lions.
2. The four gray elephants rolled the blue balls.
3. The black seals blew the shiny horns.
4. Nine clowns crawled out of the tiny car.

> ► An **adjective** is a word that describes a noun. Adjectives tell what kind or how many.

Written Practice

A. Write each sentence. Underline the nouns. Circle the adjectives.

1. Loud sirens woke up the quiet neighborhood.
2. The empty house was in flames.
3. Three trucks rushed to the blazing fire.
4. Firefighters sprayed water on the hot flames.
5. The old building burned quickly.
6. Thick smoke rolled out of the broken windows.
7. In two hours, the tired firefighters were done.
8. They rested on the cool grass before leaving.

B. Write an adjective to describe each noun.

9. boys	11. paper	13. dress	15. farm
10. tigers	12. man	14. peach	16. chalk

● **Writing Sentences**   Write four sentences. Use nouns and adjectives you wrote for exercise B.

2 | Using Adjectives

You have learned that adjectives can help you picture people, places, or things. Adjectives can also tell you exactly how something sounds, feels, tastes, or smells. Read these sentences.

> The fat worm wiggles in the dirt.
> The sticky honey is all over the table.
> The noisy cars keep me awake.
> The sour juice stings my mouth.
> The pine smell fills the room.

The worm *looks* fat. The honey *feels* sticky. The cars *sound* noisy. The juice *tastes* sour. The room *smells* of pine. The adjectives help you to see, hear, feel, taste, and smell what the sentences describe. The chart below lists some other adjectives that tell how things look, sound, feel, taste, or smell.

Look	Sound	Feel	Taste	Smell
round	loud	sharp	sweet	fresh
thin	quiet	smooth	bitter	minty
tall	squeaky	soft	salty	smoky
yellow	crying	furry	sour	flowery
happy	laughing	cold	vanilla	greasy
pretty	banging	wet	spicy	burnt

Try It Out

Give an adjective to describe each underlined noun. Use adjectives that tell how each one looks, sounds, feels, tastes, or smells.

1. The <u>food</u> made me drink a <u>glass</u> of <u>water</u>.
2. The <u>baby</u> wanted his <u>toy</u>.
3. The <u>girls</u> walked through the <u>grass</u>.
4. The <u>clerk</u> opened a <u>bottle</u> of <u>perfume</u>.
5. The <u>apples</u> spoiled in the <u>bowl</u>.

> An adjective can describe how something looks, sounds, feels, tastes, or smells.

Written Practice

Write each sentence. Add an adjective before each underlined noun. Use adjectives that tell how the noun looks, sounds, feels, tastes, or smells.

1. The <u>child</u> picked <u>flowers</u> from the <u>garden</u>.
2. The <u>class</u> looked at the <u>horse</u>.
3. <u>Clouds</u> filled the <u>sky</u>.
4. The <u>milk</u> was in a <u>glass</u>.
5. The <u>chicks</u> made <u>sounds</u>.
6. Mrs. <u>Wong</u> wore a <u>blouse</u> and <u>skirt</u>.
7. The <u>sand</u> stuck to my <u>swimsuit</u>.
8. <u>Bill</u> likes the <u>smell</u> of the <u>campfire</u>.

- **Writing a Paragraph**   Write a description of your school. Use nouns and adjectives that describe how your school looks, sounds, feels, and smells.

3 | Using *a, an,* and *the*

A, an, and *the* are adjectives you use often. *A* and *an* are used with singular nouns. *A* is used before words that begin with a consonant sound. *An* is used before words that begin with a vowel sound. Read these sentences. Listen to the beginning *sound* of each noun.

A car is parked.   An actor comes in an hour.

The can be used with both singular and plural nouns.

I saw the horse.   I saw the horses.

Try It Out

Tell whether to use *a* or *an* with each noun.

1. pen   **2.** egg   **3.** cat   **4.** ant   **5.** farm   **6.** house

---

Use *a* and *an* with singular nouns only. Use *an*
   before a word beginning with a vowel sound.
Use *a* before a word beginning with a consonant
   sound.
Use *the* with both singular and plural nouns.

Written Practice

For each noun, write *a* or *an.*

1. garden   **3.** animal   **5.** order   **7.** kite
2. flower   **4.** snowflake   **6.** hat   **8.** eye

- **Writing Sentences**   Write five sentences. Use the words above. Be sure to use *a, an,* and *the.*

4 | Comparing with Adjectives

Adjectives can describe how people, places, or things are different. Read this sentence.

Al is taller than Craig.

How is Al different from Craig? The adjective *taller* tells you one way Al is different from Craig. *Taller* compares Al's height with Craig's.

When you compare *only two* people, places, or things, the adjective usually ends with *-er*. When you compare *more than two* people, places, or things, the adjective usually ends with *-est*. Read these sentences.

Amy is shorter than Sue.
Amy is the shortest girl in the class.

The first sentence compares Amy and Sue. It compares only two people. The *-er* is added to the adjective *short*.

The second sentence compares Amy with all the other girls in the class. It compares more than two people. The *-est* ending is added to the adjective *short*.

Try It Out

Tell the correct adjective for each sentence.

1. An orange is (sweeter, sweetest) than a lemon.
2. Luis is the (older, oldest) of the three children.
3. February is (shorter, shortest) than June.
4. That tree is (taller, tallest) than this bush.
5. Rabbits are (faster, fastest) than dogs.
6. Tabby is the (smarter, smartest) of the four cats.

7. The pencil is (sharper, sharpest) than the crayon.
8. Our tree is the (taller, tallest) on our street.
9. Today is the (colder, coldest) day of the winter.
10. Your hands are (warmer, warmest) than mine.

> Adjectives that compare only two things usually
>   end with *-er*.
> Adjectives that compare more than two things
>   usually end with *-est*.

Written Practice

Write an adjective to finish each sentence. Use the word in ( ). Add *-er* if the sentence compares two nouns. Add *-est* if the sentence compares more than two nouns.

1. Today was _____ than yesterday. (cool)
2. Teng was the _____ boy in the class. (new)
3. The kitten's fur was _____ than the dog's fur. (soft)
4. Mr. Garcia is the _____ man I know. (kind)
5. The red pencil is _____ than the blue pencil. (sharp)
6. You can carry the _____ package of the four. (light)
7. Jack's coat is _____ than Charlie's jacket. (warm)
8. The brown belt is _____ than the black belt. (tight)
9. Which color do you think is the _____ of all? (dark)
10. Is Belmont Hill _____ than Grafton Hill? (high)

- **Writing Sentences** Write five sentences. In two of your sentences, compare two people, places, or things. Use adjectives with *-er*. In the other three sentences compare three people, places, or things. Use adjectives with *-est*.

5 | Using Words Correctly

to, two, too

Some words sound exactly alike, but they are spelled
differently and have different meanings. The clues in a
sentence can help you understand the meaning of the
word. Read the sentence below. Do the underlined
words sound alike?

Lee went to the kitchen.
He ate two plums, three apples, and a banana.
Lee knew he had eaten too much fruit.

Which underlined word names a number? Which
underlined word tells that there is more than enough of
something? Which underlined word means "in the
direction of?"

> To, *two*, and *too* sound alike but have different
> meanings. *To* means "in the direction of." *Two*
> names a number. *Too* means "more than
> enough."

Practice

A. Complete these sentences, using *to*, *two*, and *too*.

I ran ____ school. I forgot my ____ library
books. I have ____ much to remember. I'm just
____ sleepy this morning.

B. Write these sentences, using *to*, *two*, and *too*.

Mom took me ＿＿ her office. She also took ＿＿ of my friends. We walked ＿＿ the elevators. There were ＿＿ many buttons to push. We rode up ＿＿ floors.

there, their

There and *their* are two more words that sound alike but have different spellings and meanings. Read these sentences.

The ball is <u>there</u>. The boys said it was <u>their</u> ball.

Which underlined word tells where? Which underlined word tells that the boys own the ball?

> *There* tells where. *Their* shows ownership.

Practice

A. Use *there* and *their* to complete these sentences.

Those must be ＿＿ hats. Did I leave my hat over ＿＿? All I see are ＿＿ hats.

B. Write these sentences, using *there* and *their*.

My uncles work in the building over ＿＿. Let's go to ＿＿ bookstore. ＿＿ is a book I've wanted to read. ＿＿ bookstore is a great place. We will go ＿＿ again.

- **Writing Sentences** Write five sentences. Use *there*, *their*, *to*, *two*, and *too* in your sentences.

6 Building Vocabulary

Synonyms

Some words have almost the same meaning. Read
these sentences.

> Della was <u>happy</u> because she won the prize.
> Della was <u>glad</u> because she won the prize.

Happy and *glad* are two words that have almost the
same meaning. Such words are called **synonyms**.

> ▸ **Synonyms** are words that have almost the
> same meaning.

Practice

A. Look in the box to find a synonym for each word.

1. begin	**4.** little	look	loud
2. tell	**5.** see	small	say
3. noisy	**6.** big	large	start

B. Write a synonym for each underlined word.

7. The <u>nice</u> dog <u>moved</u> its tail.
8. The boys <u>looked</u> for the lost <u>money</u>.
9. This <u>ground</u> has a lot of <u>rocks</u> in it.
10. The children <u>went</u> to the <u>store</u>.

- **Writing Sentences**   Write two pairs of synonyms
  of your own. Use them in sentences.

Antonyms

Words that mean the opposite of each other are called **antonyms**. The underlined words in each sentence are antonyms.

The big dog has a small tail.
The happy clown has a sad face.

> ▸ **Antonyms** are words that have opposite meanings.

Practice

A. Look in the box to find an antonym for each word.

1. narrow
2. warm
3. new
4. remember

5. bad
6. first
7. wrong
8. lost

last	forget
found	cool
good	wide
right	old

B. Write an antonym for each underlined word.

9. The tall fence was painted white.
10. Jeannie won the game.
11. The wind started blowing.
12. The climbers moved up the hill.
13. The floor was clean.
14. Pat laughed until his sides hurt.
15. Rosa put on her left shoe.
16. Walt closed the door.
17. Laura was early for school.

• **Writing Sentences**   Write two pairs of antonyms of your own. Use them in sentences.

Review

- **What Is an Adjective?** *(pp. 207–208)* Write each sentence. Underline the nouns. Circle the adjectives that describe the nouns.

    1. Two friends read a good story.
    2. A young girl was carried away by a strong wind.
    3. The big wind carried her to a faraway place.
    4. She met strange people in the new land.
    5. She met a tin woodsman, a frightened lion, and a kind scarecrow.

- **Using Adjectives** *(pp. 209–210)* Write each sentence. Add adjectives to describe each underlined noun. Use adjectives that tell how the noun looks, sounds, feels, tastes, or smells.

    6. Kee had hamburgers and milk for dinner.
    7. Elaine has eyes and hair.
    8. We could hear the rain and thunder all night.
    9. Carmen loves the smell of roses.
    10. Sammy pushed the needle into the cloth.
    11. The hike on the road tired us.

- **Using *a*, *an*, and *the*** *(p. 211)* Write *a* or *an* for each noun.

12. airplane	15. van	18. aunt
13. fork	16. squirrel	19. teacher
14. jar	17. hour	20. school

- **Comparing with Adjectives** *(pp. 212–213)* Write the correct adjective for each sentence.

21. The ringmaster is the (taller, tallest) person in the circus.
22. No, the man on stilts is (taller, tallest) than the ringmaster.
23. The horse is the (faster, fastest) animal in the circus.
24. The elephant is (slower, slowest) than the horse.
25. The lion roared (louder, loudest) than the tiger.

- **Using Words Correctly** *(pp. 214–215)* Complete each sentence with the correct word.

26. (To, Too, Two) children in our class want to be animal doctors.
27. They went (to, too, two) visit an animal hospital.
28. They saw (to, too, two) animals being helped.
29. The children also went (to, too, two) the kennels.
30. They learned (to, too, two) much to remember!
31. They met kind doctors (there, their).
32. They learned how the doctors got (there, their) jobs.
33. They saw many dogs, cats, and birds (there, their).
34. The doctors let them hold (there, their) tools.
35. Now other children want to visit (there, their)!

- **Building Vocabulary** *(pp. 216–217)* Match the synonyms on the left. Match the antonyms on the right.

36. happy	**a.** thin	40. first	**a.** under
37. narrow	**b.** glad	41. young	**b.** few
38. shout	**c.** little	42. many	**c.** old
39. small	**d.** yell	43. over	**d.** last

Maintain

- **End Marks** *(p. 179)* Write each sentence. Use the correct end mark.

  1. Meg is a rock hound
  2. What is a rock hound
  3. A rock hound is a person who collects rocks
  4. Meg has more than fifty different rocks
  5. That's a lot of rocks

- **Commas in a Series** *(pp. 180–181)* Write each sentence. Use commas to separate the words in a series. If a sentence does not need commas, write *correct*.

  6. Bert Stan and Ann went on a treasure hunt.
  7. Ann found the blue box and red pencil.
  8. Bert found the seashell a comb and the soap.
  9. Stan found the chalk the button and the pine cone.
  10. There were prizes for the first second and third places.

- **Punctuation in Quotations** *(pp. 182–185)* Write each sentence. Put quotation marks, commas, and end marks in the correct places. Begin the first word of each quotation with a capital letter.

  11. Grandfather asked will you go fishing with me
  12. Paula asked will I catch a fish
  13. Grandfather answered i think you'll catch a whopper
  14. Paula asked how big is a whopper
  15. Grandfather said it can be as big as you want

- **Adjectives** *(pp. 207–213)* Write each sentence. Add an adjective to tell how each underlined noun looks, sounds, feels, tastes, or smells.

16. A blanket of snow covered the flowers.
17. The boy watched the fish swimming in the bowl.
18. We ate grapefruit and cereal.
19. The child often rides the pony.

Write the correct adjective for each sentence.

20. (The, An) brook flowed through the woods.
21. Your coat is (warmer, warmest) than mine.
22. This is the (taller, tallest) building in the city.
23. (A, An) good coach can help a team win.

- **Using Words Correctly** *(pp. 186–187, 214–215)* Write the correct word or words to complete each sentence.

24. The (to, two, too) ships sailed in the sunlight.
25. I (take, took) a picture of (there, their) colorful sails.
26. (There, Their) were many boats in the harbor.
27. I wanted (to, two, too) ride on one of them.
28. I (bring, brought) my sailing jacket.
29. I (take, took) it with me when it is cool.
30. (Bring, Brought) a scarf (to, two, too).

- **Building Vocabulary** *(pp. 216–217)* Write a synonym and an antonym for each underlined word.

31. The noisy music kept Kim awake.
32. Wayne gave his sister a big bunch of flowers.
33. The play will begin in ten minutes.
34. The tiny dog has a loud bark.

Writing a Story

1 | Telling Things in Order

Think about a story you know. What would happen if you told the story backwards? What would happen if you started in the middle? Would it make sense? The happenings in a story are told in an order that makes sense.

Every story has a beginning, a middle, and an end. The **beginning** tells who or what the story is about. The **middle** is the main part of the story. It tells what happens. The **ending** tells how the happenings in the story work out.

Read the following story. Look for the beginning, the middle, and the end.

The family of Edison Mouse was talking about their favorite cheeses. Edison's mother liked Swiss. His father liked Cheddar. Grandma Mouse liked American cheese. Uncle Pierre, who had fine tastes, liked a special cheese that sounded like "blue cheese." Edison wished he could try it.

The next week Edison was looking for something to eat in Mrs. Carter's kitchen. As he scampered across the table, he saw a big blue square with holes in it. It must be his uncle's favorite cheese, he thought.

He took a nibble. It tasted funny. If Uncle Pierre liked it, though, it must be good. Edison ate a whole corner of the cheese, then he drank some water and went home.

That night Edison was sick. His stomach was very large. Blue cheese must be fattening! Dr. Whyte Mouse gave him some medicine. Edison didn't get better.

Dr. Mouse decided to operate. During the operation, Dr. Mouse began to laugh. The nurses were shocked! The doctor held up something blue with holes in it. Edison had eaten a blue sponge!

In the story on pages 223 and 224, the first paragraph is the beginning. It tells you who the story is about—Edison. It also tells you how Edison first learns about the special cheese that leads him into a problem.

The second, third, and fourth paragraphs are the middle. They tell the main part of the story.

The last paragraph is the ending. It tells what caused Edison's problem and how his problem is solved.

Practice

Read the beginning and the ending for a story below. Write the middle of the story. Be sure you tell the things that happened in order.

Beginning

Once there was a little girl named Heather who loved to take long walks. One day Heather walked far into the woods near her house. She walked farther than she had ever walked before. Suddenly she came to a clearing. There in front of her was a whole town of tiny people and buildings!

Ending

Heather took one last look at the tiny town. She held the tiny ring tightly in her hand. Heather knew that she would always keep the ring to remind her of her very unusual day.

2 | Writing a Good Ending

The ending is an important part of every story. A good beginning catches the reader's attention. A good ending makes the story complete.

Endings can be funny or sad. Some endings may be just what you expect. Other endings may be surprises. Every ending should make the reader feel the story is finished in a way that makes sense.

Read the story below. Then read the three different endings on the next page.

Jerry's mother was sick. He wanted to take her a present when he went home from school.

Jerry wanted the present to be special. He could not buy a present because he had no money. He could draw a picture for her, but he did that often. He couldn't think of anything that was really special.

As Jerry walked home, he saw some wildflowers in a field. He decided to take his mother a bunch of the flowers, but he still wished he had something really special.

1. Jerry gave his mother the flowers when he got home. She said that she felt better just looking at them! She put them in a vase beside her bed.

2. Jerry gave his mother the flowers when he got home. He was surprised when she thanked him for two presents! Then Jerry saw a ladybug on a leaf. Jerry's mother loved ladybugs. She said that Jerry had brought her a very special present!

3. When Jerry got home, he found out his mother wasn't sick anymore. He gave her the flowers anyway.

Which ending did you expect? Which ending was boring and disappointing? Which ending surprised you? Which ending is the best?

Practice

Read the beginning and the middle for the story below. Then write two endings for the story. Decide which ending you like best.

> Kelly loved to do tricks. She could walk on her hands and turn cartwheels. She could juggle three apples and even fall down without hurting herself.
> Kelly liked to show off her tricks. Sometimes that caused problems. Once she turned a cartwheel and kicked a bag of food out of her mother's arms. The eggs in the bag were all broken. Another time Kelly smashed her little brother's new toy rocket while showing her falling trick.

3 | Getting Started

You can have your own story. Your story will be just what you want, because you will be the writer. Would you like it to be real or make-believe? Would you like it to be funny, scary, exciting, or sad?

A story has **characters.** Who would be your characters? Would they be animals or strange creatures? Would your story be about someone just like you?

A story has a **setting.** Where would you want your story to happen? Would you like the setting to be in a forest, in a faraway land, or right in your own school?

Practice

A. Decide what kind of story you like.

mystery   adventure   make-believe   real life

B. Draw a picture of a setting for your story. Then draw a picture of a character for your story. Draw as many details as you can.

C. Tell a partner a story about your pictures.

Steps for Writing a Story   Here are the steps for writing a story. You will follow these steps to write your own story.

Step One	Choose a story idea.
Step Two	Write your story.
Step Three	Revise your story.
Step Four	Proofread your story.
Step Five	Make a final copy to share.

4 | Step One
Choose a Story Idea

There are many ideas all around you that you can spin into wonderful stories. A story idea can come from a special time that you have had. A character could have exactly the same problem you had to face.

Story ideas can come from your imagination, too. Close your eyes. What imaginary land could you travel to? What imaginary animal, person, or creature could you write about?

Susan made a list of story ideas.

A woodpecker has a hard time at his new school.

A cat and a dog have an adventure together.

A girl meets a friendly giant on her way to school.

Susan got her first idea by thinking about her own first day at a new school. She got the idea for the character of this story by watching a woodpecker from the kitchen window.

She thought of her second idea when she was watching her pet cat and dog play in the yard.

She got her third idea from reading *Jack and the Beanstalk.* She decided she wanted the character in her story to meet a friendly giant instead of a mean one.

Now Susan had to decide which idea would make the best story. Susan made a chart of her ideas. By filling in the chart, she could see which topic she had the most ideas for. Read Susan's chart below.

characters: woodpecker, mother woodpecker, young animals
setting: in school
what happens: A woodpecker goes to a new school. Nobody is friendly. He's very sad. Finally he makes a new friend.

characters: cat and dog
setting: ?
what happens: They travel to strange places and have a good time.

characters: girl and giant
setting: in a city
what happens: A girl bumps into a giant. The giant is very friendly.

Susan looked over her chart. She saw that she had the most notes and details for the woodpecker story. She had an idea for an ending. The more she thought about the woodpecker, the more she knew that she could write a good story about him.

Assignment

- **Make a List**
- **Make a Chart**
- **Choose a Story Idea**

A. Make a list of story ideas.

B. Make a story chart like Susan's. Write *characters,* *setting,* and *what happens* for each story idea on your list.

C. Think about each story idea you listed. Write details on the chart. Explain who the characters are, where the setting is, and what happens.

D. Ask yourself these questions.

    1. Which story do I have the most details for?

    2. Have I thought of a good ending?

    3. Which story idea would I most enjoy writing about?

E. Choose the best idea for your story.

5 | Step Two
Write Your Story

Susan began to write her first draft. She remembered that it was important to write down her ideas first. She changed her mind about some words and sentences as she wrote. She crossed out sentences and words that she did not like. She did not worry about making mistakes. She knew that she could correct them later.

Susan's first draft

Wally is a little bird who lives in a tree. It was Wally Woodpecker's first day at a new school. Wally got up, got dressed, and went to school.

The principull showed Wally to his new classroom. Some young moles laughed at Wally's red head when he walked in.

The class read a story in the morning. Some mice rackoons made fun of the way he read. The teacher told Wally that he did a good job, but wally felt awful anyway.

When recess came, nobody wanted to play with Wally. Then Fred Fox asked Wally to play with him on the swings. Wally could push kids on swings really well. Wally felt better.

- Does Susan's story have characters and a setting?
- Does her story have a beginning, middle, and end?
- Does she tell what happened in order?
- Does it have a good ending?

Assignment • Write Your First Draft

Now it is your turn to write the first draft of your story. Remember, you may want to cross out ideas and add new and better ones. If you skip a line when you write, you will have room to make changes.

Keep these things in mind as you write your story.

1. Tell who the story is about, where it takes place, and what happened.
2. Be sure your story has a beginning, middle, and end. Write the things that happened in order.
3. Write a beginning that catches the reader's attention.
4. Write an ending that finishes the story in a way that is interesting and makes sense.

6 | Step Three
Revise Your Story

Susan read her story again. She decided that her ending wasn't very interesting or different. She wrote a new ending for her story. She liked her new ending better than the first one. She taped the new ending over her first.

Then Susan asked Pam to listen to the story. Susan wanted other ideas for making her story better. Pam enjoyed Susan's story, but Pam thought the beginning was boring. It didn't interest her in the story. Susan thought of some details she could add to the beginning to make it more lively. She wrote them between the lines on her first draft.

Susan also thought of a title for her story. She wrote it at the top of the page. She remembered where to use capital letters.

Read Susan's revised story.

Susan's revised story

Wally Shows What He Can Do

~~Wally is a little bird who lives in a tree.~~
It was Wally Woodpecker's first day at a new
school. ^His mom gave him a big breakfast of fried beetles
Wally got up, got dressed, ~~and went~~
and then she
~~to school.~~ kissed him on the beek and off he went.

The principull showed Wally to his new classroom. Some young moles laughed at Wally's red head when he walked in.

The class read a story in the morning. Some ~~mice~~ rackoons made fun of the way he read. The teacher told Wally that he did a good job, but wally felt awful anyway.

At snack time Wally sat all by himself then he saw that Fred Fox was having troble opening a can of juice. Wally offered to help. He quickley pecked a hole in the can. Fred thanked Wally and asked Wally to sit next to him. Wally gave Fred a big smile.

- What details did Susan add to the beginning?
- How did Susan make her ending better?

Assignment

- **Revise Your Story**
- **Discuss Your Story**

A. Read your story again. Underline the parts you like best.

B. Cross out any sentences that make your story boring.

C. Find at least two places where you can add more details. Write new words between the lines.

D. Write a different ending on another piece of paper. Decide which ending you like better. If you like the new ending better, tape it to your first draft.

E. Read your story to a classmate or to your teacher. Ask for ideas of other ways to make your story better. Make any changes that you think are good.

7 | Step Four
Proofread Your Story

Susan copied her story over because it was hard to read. Then she proofread it for any mistakes. Look at her first three paragraphs.

Susan's story after proofreading

> ### Wally Shows What He Can Do
>
> It was Wally Woodpecker's first day at a new school. His mom gave him a big breakfast of fried beetles. ~~and~~ T̲hen she kissed him on the
> beak
> ~~beek~~ and off he went.
> principal
> The ~~principull~~ showed Wally to his new classroom. Some young moles laughed at Wally's red head when he walked in.
> The class read a story in the morning.
> raccoons
> Some ~~rackoons~~ made fun of the way he read. The teacher told Wally that he did a good
> W
> job, but ~~wally~~ felt awful anyway.

- What spellings did Susan correct?
- Why did she make one sentence into two?
- Why did she add a capital letter?

Proofread Your Story   237

Practice

Proofread these sentences from the last paragraph of Susan's story. You will need to make four changes. Look up words you are not sure of in a dictionary. Write the corrected sentences.

At snack time Wally sat all by himself then he saw that Fred Fox was having troble opening a can of juice. Wally offered to help. He quickley pecked a hole in the can.

Assignment • Proofread Your Story

Proofread your own story. Ask yourself these questions to help you find any mistakes.

1. Are all the words spelled correctly?
2. Did I indent each paragraph?

Grammar skills checklist

3. Does each sentence tell one complete thought?
4. Does each sentence begin with a capital letter and end with the right mark?
5. Have I used capital letters for proper nouns?
6. Have I used verbs and helping words correctly?
7. Have I used pronouns correctly?

8 | Step Five
Make a Final Copy

All the students in Susan's class wanted to share their stories. They decided to make a class book. Each student could have two pages.

Susan copied her story in her best handwriting on a clean piece of paper. On a second piece of paper, she drew a picture to go with her story. The other students did the same. When they had finished, they punched three holes in the side of each page. They tied a piece of colorful yarn through the holes to hold all the pages together. When they were finished with their other work, the students could read their book of stories.

Assignment

- **Make a Final Copy**
- **Share Your Story**

A. Copy your story on a clean sheet of paper. Use your best handwriting.

B. Check your story one more time to be sure you have copied it without any mistakes.

C. Think of a special way to share your story.

- Draw a picture to go with your story. Display your story and picture on the bulletin board.
- Read your story out loud to a friend. Read it in a way that shows the feeling in the story.
- Make a class book of everyone's stories.

1 | Folktale

This African folktale explains something about the sun and the moon.

Why the Sun and the Moon Live in the Sky

Many years ago, the sun and the water were great friends. Both lived on the earth together. The sun very often used to visit the water. But the water never returned his visits.

At last, the sun asked the water why he never came to see him in his house. The water replied that the sun's house was not big enough. He said that if he came with his people, he would drive the sun out.

The water then said, "If you wish me to visit you, you must build a large house. But I warn you that it will have to be a very large place. I have many people. They take up a lot of room."

The sun promised to build a very large house. Soon afterwards, he returned to his wife, the moon. She greeted him with a broad smile.

The sun told the moon what he had promised the water. So the next day, he began building a large house in which to entertain his friend. When it was done, he asked the water to come and visit him.

When the water arrived, one of his people called out to the sun. She asked whether it would be safe for the water to enter. The sun answered, "Yes, tell my friend to come in."

The water then began to flow in with the fish and all the water animals. Very soon, the water was knee-deep. So he asked the sun if it was still safe. The sun again said, "Yes." So more of them came in.

Soon the water was level with the top of a person's head. Then the water said to the sun, "Do you want more of my people to come?"

The sun and the moon both answered, "Yes," not knowing any better. So the water people flowed on. Soon the sun and the moon had to perch themselves on top of the roof.

Again the water spoke to the sun. He received the same answer. So more of his people rushed in.

The water very soon overflowed the top of the roof. Then the sun and the moon were forced to go up into the sky. They have remained there ever since.

Elphinstone Dayrell

For Discussion

1. Many folktales explain why something is the way it is. Sometimes they are called "why" stories. How is this story like a "why" story?
2. What reason did the water give for not visiting the sun?
3. What happened when water came to visit the sun and the moon?
4. Do you think this folktale is a true story? Why or why not?

Activities

1. Write a folktale of your own that explains why something is the way it is. You might want to explain why the tiger or zebra has stripes or why the kangaroo hops.
2. Draw a picture to go with your folktale. Include all the important characters in your tale. Write the name of your folktale on your drawing.
3. Find other folktales to read in your library. Ask the librarian to help you find them.

2 | Rhyme

Here is a description in the form of a poem. In this poem, you get to add some missing words.

Summer Song

By the sand between my toes,
By the waves behind my ears,
By the sunburn on my nose,
By the little salty tears
That make rainbows in the sun   5
When I squeeze my eyes and run,
By the way the seagulls screech,
Guess where I am? *At the . . . . . !*
By the way the children shout,
Guess what happened? *School is . . . . . !*   10
By the way I sing this song,
Guess if summer lasts too long;
You must answer *Right or . . . . . !*

John Ciardi

For Discussion

1. When the lines of a poem have the same last sound, the lines **rhyme.** One pair of rhyming words in this poem is *toes* and *nose* in lines 1 and 3. Find two more pairs of words that rhyme.
2. Three of the rhymes in "Summer Song" are not complete. What do you think the missing words are?
3. In some ways poems are like songs. In fact, John Ciardi calls his poem "Summer Song." How is this poem like a song? Could you sing this poem if you wanted?
4. The poet does not say where he is, but he gives lots of clues. How many clues can you find? List them.
5. Is the poet happy or sad? Find the lines that show whether he is happy or not. Would you be happy if you were where the poet describes?

Activities

1. Draw a picture to go with this poem.
2. Write a description of one of your favorite places. It can be a forest or park or any place at all you like to visit or play. Tell what it looks like, what you do there, and how it makes you feel. Your description can be a poem if you like.

3 | Fable

Here is a special kind of story. It is called a fable. A **fable** always tells a special lesson called a moral. Read this fable and see how the moral fits.

The Fox and the Goat

A very sly fox was trapped in a well. Try as he did he could not jump out again. After a time a goat came by. When the goat saw the well, he rushed straight to the edge. "How is the water?" asked the goat.

"The water is the very best I've ever tasted!" replied the fox. "You may have some too if you like. Come on down."

The goat was very thirsty and could think of nothing but the taste of water. So down he jumped and drank his fill. But then when the goat looked around, he found that he too could not jump out.

"Let us do this," said the fox. "You stand against the wall and I will step from your back to your horns and then climb out. Then I will pull you out after me."

No sooner had they agreed to this than the fox climbed up the goat's back and pulled himself out of the well. Then the fox began walking away. The goat called after the fox so loudly that the fox returned to the well.

"You were supposed to pull me out of the well," cried the goat.

"If you had thought before you jumped in, you wouldn't have jumped in at all." The fox turned and went on his way.

Moral: Look before you leap.

For Discussion

1. Why do you think that the fox told the goat the water was the best he had ever tasted?
2. Find the sentence in the fable that tells why the goat believed the fox and jumped right in.
3. The moral in this fable is "Look before you leap." Who do you think should have learned this lesson? What are your reasons?
4. Fables often have animals in them. Why do you think that a fox was a good choice for this fable?
5. What example can you think of where you or someone you know acted like the goat or the fox in the fable?

Activities

1. Choose an animal you think might have the most interesting stories to tell. It might be a pet you have or a wild animal. Draw a cartoon for your story. Write what the characters say in speech balloons above their heads.
2. Write a fable of your own, using the same moral as the one in "The Fox and the Goat." Here is a good way to begin. "One day a ____ had a problem." Then go on to tell what the problem was and how it was solved.
3. Draw a picture to go with "The Fox and the Goat."
4. Find some other fables to read in the library. Ask your librarian to help you.

4 | Rhythm

In this poem the poet wonders about the elephant at the zoo.

Pete at the Zoo

I wonder if the elephant
Is lonely in his stall
When all the boys and girls are gone
And there's no shout at all,
And there's no one to stamp before,
No one to note his might.
Does he hunch up, as I do,
Against the dark of night?

Gwendolyn Brooks

For Discussion

1. Is Pete lonely like the elephant he is thinking about? Explain your answer.
2. You know that words that rhyme sound alike. Which lines in this poem rhyme?
3. All poems have rhythm, even if they do not rhyme. **Rhythm** is the number of beats in words. The beats in the words of the first two lines of the poem look like this.

    I wónder if the élephant

    Is lónely in his stáll

    Tap out the rhythm in the other lines of the poem.

Activities

1. Draw a picture of a zoo. Create an imaginary animal to go in it. Below the picture write one special thing your imaginary animal can do.
2. Think of an animal you might see in a zoo. Write a poem about the animal. Tell what the animal looks like or how it behaves. If you want to, make your poem rhyme.
3. Imagine that you are an animal in a zoo. Write a short poem about the people who come to see you. If you want to, draw a picture to go with your poem.

5 | Shape Poems

Some poems are written in special shapes. The shape helps you understand the poem. Read this poem by Robert Froman.

WITH THEM

COULD FLY OFF

I WISHED THAT I

INTO THE SKY

FLY OFF

SOME CROWS

ONCE I SAW

Sky Day Dream

For Discussion

1. What does the shape of "Sky Day Dream" show?
2. How does the shape add to the meaning of the poem?
3. Most poems are read from the top to the bottom. How do you read "Sky Day Dream"? Why do you think the poem is written that way?

Activities

1. Make your own shape poem. Think of an animal or a thing that would be fun to write about and draw. An elephant, a snake, or a giraffe might be good subjects for shape poems. If you make a poem about a ball, the words could go in a circle. If you tell about a giraffe, you could make the words in the shape of a horse with a very long neck.
2. Find another poem that you like. Discuss with a classmate how to make it into a shape poem. If there is an animal in the poem, you may want to write the words in the shape of the animal. If there is some action like running, you may want to make some of the words look as if they are running. When you and your classmate have a clear idea of how you want to write the poem, make a copy to share with the class.
3. Do you have a favorite song? Think of a song you have heard on the radio. Write down the words as best you can. Then, draw a picture to go with your song. Make the picture show what the song is about.

Sharing Books

Putting on a Play with Masks

Bernie read the book *A Toad for Tuesday* by Russell E. Erickson. He thought it was such a good book that he wanted to share it with his classmates.

Bernie decided to put on a play about the book using masks. He made a mask for the two main characters out of poster board. He wrote what each character would say. As he spoke each character's part, he held up a different mask in front of his face. Here is the play he presented to his class.

BERNIE: You are about to meet two characters from the book *A Toad for Tuesday* by Russell E. Erickson. One of the characters is an owl named Owl. The other is a toad named Warton.

OWL: What's your name?

WARTON: Warton.

OWL: Warton? Well, I think I'll call you Warty.

WARTON: I don't like that very much.

OWL: You don't? Well, that's too bad Warty.

WARTON: Are you going to eat me?

OWL: Am I going to eat you? Of course I'm going to eat you! Next Tuesday happens to be my birthday. A little toad will make a special birthday treat. So until that day, Warty, you may do as you please. Besides, there's no way you can possibly get down from this tree.

BERNIE: Do you think Warton gets eaten?

CLASS: No! I don't know. Yes!

BERNIE: Read the book *A Toad for Tuesday* by Russell E. Erickson to find out what happens to Warton.

- What did you find out about the characters from Bernie's play?
- Why do you think Bernie chose this part of the book to share?

Follow these steps to put on a play with masks about a book you have read.

1. Choose an interesting or exciting part of your book.
2. Write a script using your own words. You may use words the characters said in the book.
3. Make masks for each character out of poster board. Draw the shape of each mask. Next, draw places for your eyes, nose, and mouth. Then, carefully cut out your masks. Decorate the masks. Color them, and glue on pieces of fabric, feathers, and paper. Your mask does not have to look like the pictures of the characters in the book.
4. Present your play to your class. Hold the different characters' masks in front of your face. Say the characters' words. Tell the class the title and author of the book.

Activities

Here are some ways you can share a book using masks and plays.

1. Follow the steps above to put on a play using masks.
2. Write a short paragraph telling what your book is about. Write the title and author of your book. Make masks of the characters in your book. Follow the directions above. Put the masks and your paragraph on a bulletin board in your classroom.

More Books to Read

Here are some other books you may enjoy by Russell E. Erickson.

Warton and Morton   These toad brothers go on a trip and find adventure, trouble, and good things to eat.
Warton and the King of the Skies   Warton and his brother are off on an adventure in a homemade balloon. Trouble begins when they meet a pack of weasels.

2 | Making a Mobile

Terry read a book called *Mary of Mile 18* by Ann Blades. He wanted to share the book by making a mobile. Terry drew four pictures for the mobile. One picture was of something exciting that happened in the story. The other three pictures were of the characters. Here is what Terry's mobile looked like.

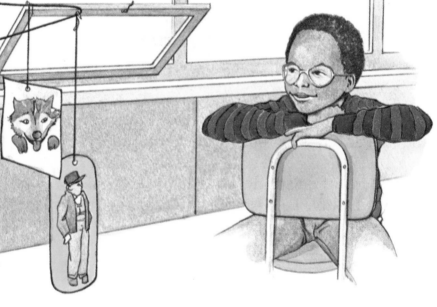

- What is the name of Terry's book?
- Who are the characters in Terry's book?
- What is one thing that happened in the book?

Follow these steps to make a mobile about a book that you have read.

1. Pick an interesting part of your book. On poster board, draw a picture of that part. If you like, you can draw on both sides of the paper.

2. Draw pictures of the main characters. Write the characters' names on the backs of the pictures. You may want to cut out the pictures.
3. Attach a piece of string to each drawing. Then tie the string to a clothes hanger.
4. Make a sign that tells the name of the book and the author's name. With string, tie the sign to the clothes hanger.

Activities

Here are some ways to share a book, using artwork.

1. Make a mobile, following the instructions above.
2. Draw a map for the book you read. Use a large piece of paper to show different places in the book. You might show the characters' houses and some important buildings. You can also show parks, forests, mountains, lakes, and beaches. Be sure to write the title of the book and the author's name on your map.
3. Use papier mâché to make a model of one or more of the characters in your book.

More Books to Read

Here are some more books about snow that you might enjoy reading.

Cross-Country Cat by Mary Calhoun   Henry the Siamese cat finds cross-country skiing to be the only way out of the mountains and back to his family.

Winter's Coming by Eve Bunting   A farm family begins to see the signs of winter.

3 | Dressing Like a Book Character

Claudine read the book *The Magic Pumpkin* by Gloria Skurzynski. Claudine dressed like a character in the book and told about the story. Here is what Claudine shared with her class.

I read a book called *The Magic Pumpkin* by Gloria Skurzynski. It is a fairy tale from India. I am dressed like Mother Parvati, a character in the book. The dress I am wearing is called a sari. A sari is a long piece of cloth that is wrapped around in a special way to make a dress.

In this story, Mother Parvati travels in a pumpkin. She gets into her pumpkin to go visit her daughter. She has to travel through the jungle where the tiger lives. The tiger thinks that he is going to catch Mother Parvati and eat her for dinner. Read the story to find out how Mother Parvati tricks the tiger.

- What did you learn about Mother Parvati?
- What did you learn about the tiger?
- What is a sari?

Follow these steps to dress like a book character.

1. Choose an important character from the book you read.
2. Dress up in old clothes, or wear your school clothes. Add a special hat or carry an object, like a baseball

bat. If your character is an animal, you can make your costume from a large paper bag. Decorate the paper bag, using crayons. Glue pieces of paper onto the bag for feathers or whiskers. Cut out holes for your arms and head.

3. Wear your costume and tell your class the title and author of your book. Tell a little about the character you are dressed as. Tell if your costume means something special in the story. Be careful not to tell too much of the story.

Activities

Here are some ways to share a book by showing what a character in the story looks like.

1. Dress like a character in your book. Follow the steps above.
2. On a large piece of paper, draw a picture of the main character in your book. Draw the character doing something exciting. Write the character's name on the paper. Also write the title of the book and the author's name.

More Books to Read

You may enjoy reading these other folktales.

The Magic Cooking Pot by Faith M. Towle   A poor man receives a magical gift from a goddess.

Why the Sun and Moon Live in the Sky by Elphinstone Dayrell and Blair Lent   The sun and the moon invite water to their house, but water brings along too many relatives.

4 | Writing a Letter About a Book

Erin knew that her friend Lisa liked stories about animals. Erin had just read *What's the Matter with Carruthers* by James Marshall. She decided to share the book by writing about it in a letter to Lisa.

Here is the letter Erin wrote.

---

102 Cresmont Lane
Falls Church, VA 22105
April 12, 1983

Dear Lisa,

Hi, Lisa. I've just read a wonderful book about a bear named Carruthers and his two friends, Eugene and Emily. It's called *What's the Matter with Carruthers* by James Marshall. Eugene is a turtle and Emily is a pig. The story is about how friends can cheer each other up. It will make you think of the things we did when one of us was feeling grumpy. I know you like stories about animals, so I think you will enjoy this one.

Your friend,
Erin

- What did Erin tell Lisa about the book?
- Why did Erin think Lisa would enjoy the book?

You can share a book by writing a letter about it.
Follow these steps.

1. Choose a book that you like and one you think your friend will like.
2. In your letter, write the title of the book and the author's name.
3. Tell a little about the characters and what happens in the book. Do not tell too much.
4. Explain why you liked the book. Tell your friend why you think he or she will enjoy the book.

Activities

1. Using the directions above, write a letter about a book you have read.
2. Write to the author of a book you liked. Thank the author for writing such a good story. Be sure to tell the author why you liked the book. You might tell what your favorite part of the book is.

More Books to Read

Here are other books by James Marshall you might enjoy reading.

The Guest   Mona Moose learns at last why her house guest, Maurice Snail, left so suddenly.

Speedboat   Jasper and his best friend have funny adventures in a speedboat and at home.

A Summer in the South   Someone is trying to scare Marietta Chicken, who is spending the summer at a seaside hotel. The famous detective Elenor Owl solves the case.

5 | Interviewing a Book Character

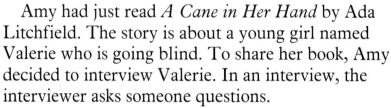

Amy had just read *A Cane in Her Hand* by Ada Litchfield. The story is about a young girl named Valerie who is going blind. To share her book, Amy decided to interview Valerie. In an interview, the interviewer asks someone questions.

Amy wrote down the interviewer's questions and the character's answers. Amy only asked questions that could be answered by things that happened in the book. Amy asked a classmate to be the interviewer. She would play the part of Valerie.

Here is the interview Amy presented to her class.

INTERVIEWER: Valerie, how did you feel when you found out that you were going blind?

VALERIE: I was very scared. I had already had operations, and there was nothing more the doctor could do.

INTERVIEWER: Did you have problems getting around?

VALERIE: Oh yes, the biggest problem I had was that I kept bumping into things, especially at school.

INTERVIEWER: What did you do about that?

VALERIE: I had to learn new ways of getting around. I went to a special teacher for students who do not see very well. Miss Sousa taught me how to use a cane and many other things.

INTERVIEWER: To find out more about Valerie, read *A Cane in Her Hand* by Ada Litchfield.

- How did you learn about the character in the book?
- What did you find out about the character?
- What kinds of questions did the interviewer ask?

To interview a character in a book you read, follow these steps.

1. Choose an important character from your book.
2. Write what the interviewer will ask and what the character will answer.
3. Ask the character questions only about what happened in the story.
4. Answer the questions as you think the character would.
5. Ask a classmate to read the interviewer's questions. You be the character.
6. Present your interview to your class. Remember to tell the title and author of the book.

Activities

Here are ways to share a book by interviewing.

1. Interview a character from a book that you have read, following the steps above.
2. Interview two classmates who read a book they liked. Ask them the title and author of the book. Find out why they like the book and who their favorite characters are.

More Books to Read

Here are some other books you may enjoy about people with physical problems.

Anna's Silent World by Bernard Wolf   A young deaf girl leads a fun-filled and active life.
Tracy by Nancy Mack   In spite of her cerebral palsy, Tracy gets along at home and at school.

End-of-Book Test

- **Sentences**   Write another sentence by changing the order of the words. Label the new sentence *S* for statement, *Q* for question, or *E* for exclamation.

    1. Mario took his dog for a walk.
    2. The dog saw a fox.
    3. Will the dog chase the fox?
    4. How fast the dog chases the fox!

- **Subjects and Predicates**   Write each sentence. Put a line between the subject and the predicate.

    5. The river overflowed its banks.
    6. The people left their homes quickly.
    7. Boats carried some people to dry land.

- **Separating Sentences**   Rewrite the story below by separating the sentences. Begin each sentence with a capital letter. End each sentence with the correct mark.

    Lorna put on her skates she skated to the center of the ice. Lorna skated to the music then she slipped and fell. She stood up and started skating again the people clapped and cheered.

- **Common and Proper Nouns**   Write the nouns in each sentence. Write *C* after the common nouns. Write *P* after the proper nouns.

    8. Mrs. Avery lives in New England.
    9. She has a vegetable garden near her house.
    10. In July her grandchildren from Chicago came.

- **Singular and Plural Nouns**   Write the plural form of each noun.

  11. cherry   **13.** tooth   **15.** woman   **17.** tent
  12. match   **14.** brush   **16.** foot   **18.** mouse

- **Nouns That Show Ownership**   Change the underlined words to a noun that shows ownership.

  19. umbrella of the woman
  20. ears of the rabbits
  21. toys of the children
  22. aunt of Peter
  23. cage of the mice
  24. chair of Grandfather

- **Abbreviations**   Write the abbreviation of each word.

  25. Tuesday   **26.** September   **27.** Wednesday

- **Verbs**   Write each sentence. Put a line between the subject and the predicate. Draw one line under the verb.

  28. A fog rolled in from the ocean.
  29. Emily and Will walked to the shore.
  30. They watched a boat in the fog.
  31. The boat moved very slowly.

- **Verbs in the Present**   Write the correct present time verb in ( ) for each sentence.

  32. Gina and Frank (decorate, decorates) the room.
  33. Frank (push, pushes) the chair against the wall.
  34. Gina (carry, carries) a large painting.
  35. Frank (plug, plugs) in a lamp cord.

- **Verbs in the Past**   Write the past time of the verb in
  ( ) to complete each sentence.

  36. The cafeteria ____ on the sixth floor. (is)
  37. Janet ____ the elevator button. (press)
  38. She ____ her salad dressing. (mix)
  39. She ____ her tray to a table. (carry)

- **Contractions with *not***   Write the contraction for
  each pair of words.

40. would not	**42.** has not	**44.** will not
41. is not	**43.** were not	**45.** have not

- **Pronouns**   Write the pronoun or pronouns in each
  sentence. Write *S* if the pronoun is in the subject. Write
  P if the pronoun is in the predicate.

  46. Hilda and I are getting ready for the party.
  47. We have invited Preston, Louise, and Ronald.
  48. They will bring Edward with them.
  49. He will bring a costume with him.
  50. The costume is too small for me now.

- ***I* and *me***   Write the sentence, using *I* or *me* in the
  blank.

  51. Marvin is going on a hike with Judy and ____.
  52. Judy and ____ will pack a lunch.
  53. Marvin gave his lunch to ____.
  54. ____ know where the trail leads.

- **Contractions**   Write a contraction for each pair of
  words.

55. we are	**58.** they have	**61.** we will
56. he is	**59.** she will	**62.** you have
57. I am	**60.** you are	**63.** they are

266   **End-of-Book Test**

- **Punctuation** Write each sentence. Put capital letters, quotation marks, commas, and end marks in the correct places.

64. Norman asked are you going to watch television
65. Joy answered no, I have to do my homework
66. Norman said i'm finished with my homework
67. Joy replied i'll be finished in a little while

- **Commas in a Series** Write each sentence. Put commas in the correct places in the series.

68. The zoo is open on Thursday Friday and Saturday.
69. We saw storks flamingoes and ducks at the zoo.
70. Parrots canaries and eagles are my favorite birds.
71. Monkeys eat nuts bananas and other fruits.

- **Adjectives** Write each sentence. Underline the nouns. Circle the adjectives that describe the nouns.

72. The bright sun shone on the dry desert.
73. The little animals hid from the hot sun.
74. The long train had twenty cars.
75. The large wheels made a loud noise.
76. The tired boy looked at the clean windows.
77. The happy people passed beautiful scenery.

- **Using *a*, *an*, and *the*** Write the adjectives in ( ) that complete the sentences correctly.

78. Have you ever built (a, an) sand castle?
79. (An, The) beach is (an, the) best place to build one.
80. Maria has built (a, an) unusual castle.
81. All (a, the) children want to see (an, the) castle.
82. (A, The) author received (a, an) award for writing the book.
83. (An, The) book was about lizards.

- **Comparing with Adjectives**   Write the correct adjective in ( ) for each sentence.

84. A sparrow is (smaller, smallest) than an owl.
85. The hummingbird is the (smaller, smallest) bird.
86. A hawk flies (faster, fastest) than a sparrow.
87. What is the world's (larger, largest) bird?

- **Using Words Correctly**   Write the word in ( ) that correctly completes the sentence.

88. Mr. Brady has (gone, went) to work.
89. He (did, done) some chores before he left.
90. What chores has he (did, done)?
91. He has (wrote, written) a note for Mrs. Brady.
92. The newspaper (came, come) at six o'clock.
93. The girl (ran, run) to the front door.
94. She had (ran, run) from the corner.
95. Jerry (bring, brought) the newspaper to school.
96. He (gave, given) the paper to the teacher.
97. I have (saw, seen) the newspaper already.
98. I have (bring, brought) the newspaper inside.
99. Ellen (saw, seen) the paper, too.
100. Ellen's family has (ate, eaten) breakfast already.
101. Ellen (took, taken) the paper out of the wrapper.

- **Using Word Clues**   Write the meaning of the underlined word in each sentence. Use the clues in the sentence to help you.

102. The <u>resounding</u> bell hurt the dog's ears.
    a. loud   **b.** pretty
103. The <u>dense</u> bushes were so close together that she couldn't walk through them.
    a. green   **b.** thick

- **Compound Words** Write the compound words in these sentences. Then draw a line between the two words that make up the compound.

  104. The movie was about spaceships.
  105. Sunlight shone on the grapevines.
  106. Your handwriting is easy to read.

- **Prefixes and Suffixes** Write the meaning of each underlined word.

  107. The story was <u>unbelievable</u>.
  108. We will have to <u>rewrite</u> it.
  109. The <u>climber</u> reached the top of the mountain.
  110. The search seemed <u>hopeless</u>.

- **Sound Words** Write a sound word that describes each group of words below.

  111. the sound a cat makes
  112. the sound a clock makes
  113. rain on the roof
  114. a plane taking off

- **Synonyms** Write a synonym for each underlined word.

  115. Ramona <u>completed</u> her work.
  116. We were standing very <u>near</u> to him.
  117. The team was ready to <u>begin</u> the game.

- **Antonyms** Write an antonym for each underlined word.

  118. The math problem was <u>difficult</u> to do.
  119. The glass was <u>empty</u>.
  120. Henry sat on the <u>hard</u> chair.

Language Handbook

Parts of Speech

Nouns

Definition   A noun names a person, place, or thing.

The <u>players</u> rode the <u>bus</u> across <u>town</u>.

Practice   Copy each sentence. Underline each noun.

1. The farmer ordered some seeds.
2. The package came to the house.
3. The plants are in small boxes.
4. The plow gets the field ready.

Singular and Plural Nouns   **Singular nouns** name one person, place, or thing. **Plural nouns** name more than one person, place, or thing.

A <u>woman</u> rode her <u>bike</u> to <u>town</u>. (singular)
Some <u>women</u> drove <u>cars</u> to the <u>stores</u>. (plural)

Practice   Copy each sentence. Put one line under each singular noun. Put two lines under each plural noun.

1. A baby seal is a pup.
2. Some seals lay on the rocks.
3. One old seal barked at the gulls.
4. A boat went past the island.
5. All the passengers startled the seals.

Most singular nouns are made plural by adding -*s*.

picture–pictures shovel–shovels

Singular nouns ending with -*es*, -*ch*, -*sh*, or -*x* are made plural by adding -*es*.

bus–buses dish–dishes fox–foxes match–matches

Some singular nouns that end with -*y* are made plural by changing the -*y* to -*i*, and then adding -*es*.

party–parties spy–spies

Some nouns are made plural by changing the spelling.

mouse–mice child–children

Practice Copy each singular noun. Then write its plural form.

1. wish
2. gerbil
3. fox

4. pony
5. patch
6. loss

Common and Proper Nouns A **common noun** names any person, place, or thing. A **proper noun** names a particular person, place, or thing. Proper nouns begin with capital letters.

The <u>man</u> patted the <u>kitten</u>. (common)
<u>Uncle Ollie</u> patted <u>Tigger</u>. (proper)

Practice Write the nouns. Write *C* after each common noun. Write *P* after each proper noun.

1. The boys went to town.
2. Alfred and Wayne went to Medford.
3. What day is the party?
4. Come to my house on Thursday.

Nouns That Show Ownership   Some nouns show that something belongs to the owner.

a <u>boy's</u> dog   a <u>dog's</u> collar   a <u>team's</u> park

Most singular nouns show ownership by adding an apostrophe and *-s* (*-'s*) to the end of the noun.

Matina's bike   my mother's book

Most plural nouns show ownership by adding *only* an apostrophe after the *s*.

some girls' coats   the nations' flags

Practice   Write each noun that shows ownership. Write *S* after each singular noun that shows ownership. Write *P* after each plural noun that shows ownership.

1. On my cousin's birthday we went to the zoo.
2. The animals' dinners were being prepared.
3. An elephant's keeper showed us around.
4. We walked over to some giraffes' cages.
5. A baby panda snuggled against the mother's fur.

Abbreviations   An **abbreviation** is a short way of writing a word. An abbreviation usually ends with a period. Abbreviations of proper nouns begin with capital letters.

Tuesday-Tues. Wednesday-Wed. January-Jan.
March-Mar.   August-Aug.   Friday-Fri.

Practice   Write the abbreviation for each word below.

1. Monday
2. April
3. Saturday
4. September
5. December
6. Thursday

Verbs

Definition   A **verb** is a word that shows action.

The robin <u>ate</u> a raisin.
Alice <u>opened</u> the letter.

Practice   Copy each sentence. Underline each verb.

1. The water gurgled in the drain.
2. A frog croaked.
3. I see a bus.
4. The store closes at six o'clock.
5. The mail arrives early on Saturday.

Verbs in the Present   Verbs in the **present time** tell that an action is happening now.

The astronauts <u>land</u> safely. Millions of people <u>watch</u>.

With a singular subject, verbs in the present end with -*s*. With a plural subject, verbs in the present do not end with -*s*.

Jerry walks to school. (singular subject)
The doors open at eight. (plural subject)

Verbs in the present that end with -*s*, -*sh*, -*ch*, or -*x* add -*es* when used with singular subjects.

The car passes.
The snowplow pushes.
The cook mixes.

Verbs in the present that end with a consonant and -*y* change the *y* to *i* and add -*es* when used with singular subjects.

Rita hurries to school.

Practice Read each sentence. Write *S* if the subject is singular. Write *P* if the subject is plural. Then write the correct verb for each sentence.

1. The train (arrive, arrives) at noon.
2. The passengers (rush, rushes) out of the station.
3. My grandfather (carry, carries) his suitcases.
4. The suitcases (match, matches).

Verbs in the Past Verbs in the **past time** show that an action has already happened.

We camp every summer. We <u>camped</u> last year.

Many verbs show past time by adding -*ed*.

Some children walk to school. We walked yesterday.

Verbs ending with -*e* drop the final -*e* and add -*ed* to show past time.

Babies often gurgle. The baby gurgled this morning.

Verbs ending with a consonant and -*y* change the *y* to *i* and add -*ed.*

Some people hurry all day. Jeff hurried home late last night.

Practice Read each sentence. Write *present* if the verb shows present time. Write *past* if the verb shows past time.

1. The puppies crawl over each other.
2. Their mother licked them.
3. One puppy chases a bug.
4. The bug flies away.
5. The mother carried the pup home.

Special Verbs *Am, are, is, was,* and *were* are **special verbs.** They do not take the endings *-s* or *-ed.*

There were clouds in the sky. It was dark. Now the sun is out. I am glad. We are in the sunshine again.

Practice Write the correct verb for each sentence. Then write *present* if the verb shows present time. Write *past* if the verb shows past time.

1. The seagulls (is, are) on the beach.
2. Last night they (are, were) on the roof.
3. One gull (is, am) squawking now.
4. It (was, were) fun to watch the gulls last summer.
5. I (are, am) interested in their habits.

Contractions with *not* A **contraction** is one word made by putting two words together and shortening them. Put an apostrophe (') in place of any letters dropped to make the contraction.

Nan was not home.   Don could not come.
Nan wasn't at home.   Don couldn't come.

Practice Write the contractions for the underlined words.

1. These vegetables <u>do not</u> look fresh.
2. I <u>would not</u> want to eat them.
3. They <u>cannot</u> have many vitamins.
4. I <u>will not</u> buy them.
5. It <u>does not</u> seem wise.

Pronouns

Definition   A **pronoun** is a word used in place of a noun or nouns.

Ned has a bike. He takes good care of it.
The wind blew hard. It blew down the tree.

I, you, he, she, it, we, and *they* are pronouns.

Jan is a painter.   Michael read a story to Judy.
She is a painter.   He read a story to Judy.

Other pronouns that take the place of nouns are *me, him, her, us,* and *them.*

Joe waved to Tia and Dom.   The letter is for Ann.
Joe waved to them.   The letter is for her.

Practice   Change the underlined words in each sentence to a pronoun. Write the new sentence.

1. The girls hurried to catch the subway.
2. Mary and I waved to the conductor.
3. The conductor stopped the train.
4. Dad took Erica and me to the skating rink.

Adjectives

Definition   An **adjective** describes a noun.

seven goats   winter hats   comfortable chairs

Adjectives tell what kind or how many.

three rugs   open doors   frightened mice

An adjective can describe how something looks, feels, sounds, tastes, or smells.

a sweet scent   a loud noise   a wide street

Practice Read these sentences. Write each adjective and the noun it describes. Underline the adjective.

1. We saw orange buses.
2. Four children sang songs.
3. Angry drivers honked loud horns.
4. Friendly drivers waved to us.
5. Two buses carried sixty children.

Using *a*, *an*, and *the* *A, an,* and *the* are **adjectives.**

An anteater and a panda are in the zoo.

The adjectives *a* and *an* are used with singular nouns only. Use *an* before a word beginning with a vowel sound. Use *a* before a word beginning with a consonant sound.

a child   a trip   a banana   a turnip
an uncle   an ape   an orange   an envelope

The is used with singular or plural nouns.

the kite   the mule   the wooden door
the kites   the mules   the wooden doors

Practice Write each noun. Write *a* or *the* in front of the words in 1, 2, and 3. Write *a* or *an* in front of the words in 4, 5, and 6.

1. marbles
2. pigs
3. pennies
4. umbrella
5. necklace
6. oven

Adjectives That Compare Some **adjectives** are used to **compare** two or more things.

The tree is taller than the house.
This is the oldest house on the street.

Adjectives that compare only two things usually end with -er.

Tony is younger than George.
The truck is bigger than the van.

Adjectives that compare more than two things usually end with -est.

Jill caught the biggest fish.
This is the longest trip I've ever taken.

Practice Read each sentence. Write the correct adjective.

1. Today is (warmer, warmest) than yesterday.
2. The sky is the (bluer, bluest) I have ever seen.
3. Irma types (faster, fastest) than Libby.
4. Armando types the (faster, fastest) of all.
5. My blue shirt is (newer, newest) than my green one.

Contractions with Pronouns A **contraction** can be made by joining a pronoun and a verb. To make the contraction, use an apostrophe in place of the letter or letters that are left out.

I am here.   We will go.   It is a school day today.
I'm here.   We'll go.   It's a school day today.

Practice Read each sentence. Put a contraction in place of the underlined words. Write the new sentences.

1. She is my friend.
2. We have been friends for years.
3. You are our neighbor.
4. They are leaving now.
5. I will be home soon.

Sentences

The Sentence

Definition   A **sentence** is a group of words that tells a complete thought. A sentence begins with a capital letter and ends with a punctuation mark.

My dog is barking.
A cat is on the porch.

Practice   Copy each group of words that is a sentence.

1. Marie went to the market.
2. In the shopping center.
3. She filled the cart.
4. There was a long line.
5. She drove home.
6. Carried the bags inside.

Word Order   Changing **word order** can change sentence meaning.

A <u>bus</u> honked at the <u>car</u>.
A <u>car</u> honked at the <u>bus</u>.

Practice   Change the word order. Write the new sentences.

1. A man bit a dog.
2. Tish is larger than Tony.
3. Mother carried the bag for Janet.
4. My cousin lives with my aunt.
5. Jake went to see Sam.
6. The children had a surprise for the teacher.

Separating Sentences   Do not run sentences together. Start each sentence with a capital letter. End with the correct mark.

Jane came inside she sat down. (run together)
Jane came inside. She sat down. (separated)

Practice   Copy the story. Use a capital letter to start each sentence. End each sentence with the correct mark.

Chandra is dancing Will is dancing too it is fun. The teacher dances with them she says they dance very well would you like to try it, too

Subjects and Predicates   Every sentence has a **subject** and a **predicate**. The **subject** tells who or what the sentence is about. The **predicate** tells what the subject does or is.

The soup is hot. (subject)
Mehalia and Julio ate some. (subject)
Brad fixed sandwiches. (predicate)
My sandwich is egg salad. (predicate)

Practice   Copy each sentence. Draw one line under the subject. Draw two lines under the predicate.

1. The front door slammed.
2. Emily and her father walked down the street.
3. Dinner is ready.
4. These three letters arrived today.
5. This old house is made of stone.
6. All the windows rattled.
7. The girl and the boy played in the park with the dog.

Kinds of Sentences

Statements, Questions, and Exclamations A
sentence that tells something is a **statement**. A
statement ends with a period (.). A sentence that asks
something is a **question**. A question ends with a
question mark (?). A sentence that shows strong feeling
is an **exclamation**. An exclamation ends with an
exclamation mark (!).

Molly will go to camp. (statement)
Will Charles go to camp? (question)
It will be wonderful! (exclamation)

Practice Copy each sentence. Add the punctuation
marks.

1. Vernon went for a walk
2. Where did he go
3. It is getting cold and windy
4. Here comes the rain
5. Do you think that Vernon will get wet
6. He did not wear boots
7. Did he take a jacket
8. Vernon is coming now
9. Look at him run

Using Words Correctly

ate, eaten   Use the helping word *has* or *have* with *eaten. Ate* does not need a helping word.

The kitten <u>ate</u> the food. It <u>has</u> not <u>eaten</u> much today.

bring, brought   Use *bring* or *brings* in the present. Use *brought* in the past.

We <u>bring</u> home our work. Martha <u>brings</u> her skates. They <u>brought</u> their sleds over yesterday.

came, come   Use the helping word *has* or *have* with *come. Came* does not need a helping word.

I <u>came</u> home early, but Dad <u>has</u> not <u>come</u> yet.

did, done   Use the helping word *has* or *have* with *done. Did* does not need a helping word.

We <u>have done</u> our work. We <u>did</u> it well.

gave, given   Use the helping word *has* or *have* with *given. Gave* does not need a helping word.

I <u>gave</u> John a gift. I <u>have given</u> it to him already.

gone, went   Use the helping word *has* or *have* with *gone. Went* does not need a helping word.

My sister <u>has gone</u> to the dentist. She <u>went</u> early this morning.

I, me   When you speak of yourself, use *I* in the subject of the sentence. Use *me* in the predicate of the sentence. Whenever you speak of yourself and another person, it is polite to name yourself last.

Andy and <u>I</u> / went to a show. Andy / met <u>me</u> at the theater.

ran, run   Use the helping word *has* or *have* with *run*. *Ran* does not need a helping word.

The clock <u>ran</u> for a week, but now it <u>has run</u> down.

saw, seen   Use the helping word *has* or *have* with *seen*. *Saw* does not need a helping word.

Who <u>has seen</u> the movie? Rhoda <u>saw</u> it before.

there, their   *There* tells where. *Their* shows ownership.

Put it over <u>there</u>. The neighbors lost <u>their</u> dog.

to, two, too   *To* means "in the direction of." *Two* names a number. *Too* means "more than enough."

I walked <u>to</u> a store. I bought <u>two</u> pens. They cost <u>too</u> much.

took, taken   Use the helping word *has* or *have* with *taken*. *Took* does not need a helping word.

A squirrel <u>took</u> the nuts. It <u>has taken</u> them away.

wrote, written   Use the helping word *has* or *have* with *written*. *Wrote* does not need a helping word.

I <u>wrote</u> to Aunt Nell. I <u>have</u> <u>written</u> to Uncle Oz too.

Practice   Read each sentence. Write the word or words to complete each sentence.

1. After we (ate, eaten) we (did, done) the dishes.
2. Ned (bring, brought) a ball when he (came, come).
3. Marissa (gave, given) a pencil case to (I, me).
4. Have you (run, ran) all the way (to, two, too) school?
5. Ralph has (saw, seen) the movie we (gone, went) to.
6. Someone (took, taken) (their, there) car.

Punctuation and Capitalization

Punctuation

End Marks   The period (.), the question mark (?), and the exclamation mark (!) are end punctuation marks.

It's raining! How do you know? I looked outside.

Commas in a Series   Three or more words listed together are a **series.** Commas separate words in a series.

We played with Jack, Ginny, and Fred.
We brought a bat, a ball, and a mitt.

Practice   Copy each sentence. Add the punctuation.

1. Is someone outside
2. I will look out the window
3. Why, Grandpa is here
4. We planted maple elm oak and pine trees
5. Alex put the sheets blankets and quilt on his bed

Using Quotation Marks   A speaker's exact words are called a **quotation.** Use **quotation marks** (" ") at the beginning and end of a quotation.

Nora said, "It's my birthday."
Henry said, "It's mine, too!"

Punctuating Quotations   Use a comma to separate the exact quotation from the rest of the sentence. Begin the first word of a quotation with a capital letter. Put the end mark inside the last quotation mark.

Pia said, "We will help you."
Elise asked, "Where is Nick?"

Practice   Copy each sentence. Use capital letters and punctuation marks correctly.

1. Eric said this is a starfish
2. Angel asked where did you find it
3. Joan exclaimed the clock has stopped
4. Tina asked what time is it
5. Ed replied it is nearly two o'clock

Capitalization

Sentences   Every sentence begins with a capital letter.

There are some books. They belong to Joe.

Quotations   A quotation begins with a capital letter.

Nia said, "The doorbell just rang."
Jay asked, "Who's there?"

Proper Nouns   A proper noun begins with a capital letter. If a proper noun has more than one word, each important word begins with a capital letter.

Samantha   Africa   Museum of Science

Abbreviations of Proper Nouns   The abbreviation of a proper noun begins with a capital letter.

Fri., Jan. 6, 1927

Practice   Copy each sentence. Use capital letters correctly.

1. there is a package for jack willard.
2. helen said, "give it to him now."
3. the address on the package is avery road.
4. raymond asked, "where is vassar street?"

More Practice

- **What Is a Sentence?**   Write the group of words that makes a complete sentence.

  1. Ride in a car.
     I like to ride in a car.
  2. The front seat is best.
     The best seat.
  3. Out the window.
     I look out the window.
  4. Cars zoom by me.
     Zoom by.
  5. Up the hills.
     We go up the hills.
  6. At people.
     I wave at people.

- **Word Order**   Write another sentence by changing the order of the words.

  7. Ed stepped into the boat ahead of Cora.
  8. After they rode upstream, they went fishing for rainbow trout.
  9. The motorboat hit a big wave.
  10. Was Ed more frightened than Cora?
  11. Cora sees a moose on the shore.
  12. The river is deeper than the lake.

- **Statements, Questions, and Exclamations**   Write each sentence. Use the correct end mark.

  13. I can keep a secret
  14. What a secret it is
  15. Lynn told Jeffrey her secret
  16. Jeffrey did not keep the secret
  17. Why did Jeffrey give away the secret

- **Subjects and Predicates**   Write each sentence. Put a line between the subject and the predicate.

18. Louis builds model airplanes in his spare time.
19. His sister Rachel likes to climb trees.
20. The weather is damp and rainy today.
21. Louis and Rachel build model airplanes together.
22. Uncle Al watches them.
23. They can hear the rain on the roof.

- **Separating Sentences**   Separate each group of sentences below. Begin each sentence with a capital letter. End each sentence with the correct mark.

24. Our family likes to tell stories some of the stories are about about me.
25. Some of the stories are funny my dad tells about being a little boy.
26. Does your family tell stories maybe you hear the same stories many times.
27. My uncle tells the best stories they are about being a sailor.

Enrichment

Play this sentence-building game with four or more of your classmates. One person begins by saying a word (for example, *The*). The next player repeats the word and adds another (*The brown*). The next player repeats the two words and adds a third (*The brown horse*). The game continues until a complete sentence has been made. If a player does not repeat the words correctly or uses a word that does not make sense, he or she is out.

Play the game several times. Write down the sentences you make. Draw pictures to go with them.

More Practice

- **Common and Proper Nouns**   Write the nouns in each sentence. Put a *P* next to the proper nouns. Put a *C* next to the common nouns.

    1. The racetrack is in Middletown.
    2. Many drivers bring cars to Middletown Racetrack.
    3. Martin is the fastest racer.
    4. Martin calls his car "The Flying Spirit."
    5. The first prize is a trip to Hawaii.

- **Singular and Plural Nouns**   Change the spelling of these singular nouns to make them plural.

6. vegetable	**8.** goose	**10.** city	**12.** foot
7. patch	**9.** bush	**11.** child	**13.** fox

- **Nouns That Show Ownership**   Write a sentence making each underlined word show ownership.

14. the name of the <u>girl</u>	**18.** bike of my <u>brother</u>
15. the book of the <u>child</u>	**19.** the coats of the <u>boys</u>
16. paws of the <u>monkeys</u>	**20.** cribs of the <u>babies</u>
17. stem of the <u>plant</u>	**21.** store of the <u>women</u>

- **Abbreviations**   Write an abbreviation for each underlined word in this paragraph.

    Carmen Rivera is celebrating her birthday today. It is <u>Friday</u>, <u>October</u> 10. She received birthday cards on <u>Thursday</u> from Juan Navarro and Maria Garcia.

Juan's birthday was on <u>Monday</u>. Maria's birthday
will be in <u>January</u>. Carmen has not seen Maria
Garcia since last <u>August</u>.

- **Using Words Correctly**   Write each sentence. Use
the correct word in ( ).

22. Richard (did, done) his work near the river.
23. Maggie has (wrote, written) about the water.
24. Paul has (did, done) his homework.
25. Mollie (wrote, written) on the chalkboard.

- **Building Vocabulary**   Complete each sentence by
making a compound word from the two lists in the box.

26. The door wouldn't open
because the ____ was
missing.
27. Have you ridden on a
Mississippi River ____?
28. Her ____ is easy to read.
29. The tomatoes ripened in
the ____ .

hand	boat
sun	writing
steam	knob
door	light

Enrichment

On a large paper, make a chart that looks like this.

	Persons	Places	Things
COMMON NOUNS			
PROPER NOUNS			

Read three or four pages from one of your favorite
stories. Find all the nouns on those pages. Put them in
the right places in the chart. Have a friend check to see
if he or she agrees with your choices.

More Practice

- **What Is a Paragraph?** Remember that a paragraph is a group of sentences that are all about one main idea. Read this paragraph.

    Yesterday Dad and I made mint tea. First, we picked the mint and rinsed it off under cold water. We put the mint leaves into a big teapot. Next, we boiled a kettle of water. Then we poured very hot water over the leaves and waited. When the water had cooled down, our mint tea was ready.

Write the main idea of the paragraph above.

a. You boil water to make tea.
b. This is how to make mint tea.
c. Mint makes good tea.

Roberta wrote the following sentences to use in a paragraph about putting her baby brother to bed. Write the numbers of the sentences that do *not* tell about the main idea.

1. Sometimes my mother lets me get my baby brother ready for bed.
2. Sometimes I give him breakfast, too.
3. First, I give him a bath and put pajamas on him.
4. Next, I tuck him into bed and read him a story.
5. When he falls asleep, I turn off the light.
6. I hold his hand when we go shopping.
7. Then I tiptoe out of his room.

- **Topic Sentences**   A topic sentence is usually the first sentence of a paragraph. It tells what the paragraph is about.

  The paragraph below does not have a topic sentence. Read the paragraph. Then write a good topic sentence for it.

    Mrs. Martinez lets children play in her yard. She lets her neighbors borrow her garden tools. She helps people when they are sick. She remembers everyone's birthday. She feeds birds and animals.

- **Order in Paragraphs**   Below are steps for making a telephone call from a phone booth. The steps are out of order. Write the steps in order as a paragraph.

  Follow these steps for making a phone call.
  Finally, give your name and tell why you are calling.
  Second, put a coin in the slot.
  Then dial the number.
  First, find the right number in the telephone book.

  The order words *first, second, then,* and *finally* gave you clues in the sentences above. Write your own paragraph telling how to make a sandwich. Use order words to guide your reader through the steps.

- **Proofreading**   There are two mistakes in each sentence below. Write each sentence correctly. If you are not sure about a spelling, check a dictionary.

  1. A macaw is a kind of parrat
  2. this bird has butiful feathers.
  3. it has a very long tail
  4. a macaw makes a harsh noyse.
  5. It may live mor than sixty year.

More Practice

- **What Is a Verb?**   Write each sentence. Put a line between the subject and predicate. Draw one line under the verb.

    1. Claudia took a trip to Egypt.
    2. She rode a camel.
    3. Her sister Libby went with her.
    4. Libby wrote letters.
    5. The girls flew home in an airplane.

- **Verbs in the Present**   Write the correct verb for each sentence.

    6. Koalas (live, lives) in Australia.
    7. The koala (clutch, clutches) onto branches.
    8. The mother koala (carry, carries) her young cub in her pouch.
    9. The koala (eat, eats) the leaves of the blue gum tree.
    10. It also (dig, digs) up the roots from the ground to eat.

- **Verbs in the Past**   Write the past time of the word in ( ) to complete each sentence.

    11. The wind ____ through the trees. (whistle)
    12. The rain ____ against the windows. (splash)
    13. A cat ____ in the rain. (cry)
    14. Betty ____ the front door. (open)
    15. The cat ____ into the warm kitchen. (walk)

- **Special Verbs**   Write the correct verb for each sentence.

  16. The lights (is, are) turned off.
  17. The door (is, are) locked.
  18. It (was, were) time to leave for vacation.
  19. The Martins (was, were) going to the mountains.

- **Contractions with *not***   Write the contraction for each pair of words.

  20. did not   22. have not   24. do not
  21. were not   23. should not   25. cannot

- **Using Words Correctly**   Write the correct word to complete each sentence.

  26. Dina had (run, ran) to work.
  27. The buses (run, ran) late all week.
  28. She (come, came) home early this evening.
  29. The bus has (come, came) on time for once!

Enrichment

Below is a list of words that can be used as verbs. Choose any four verbs from the list. Then write one sentence for each verb you chose. You may use any verb form you wish. Try to make your sentences tell a story. Use a dictionary if you need to.

wiggle	work	drift
squeak	call	pump
splash	roar	eat
tell	catch	chase
whisper	struggle	run

More Practice

- **Using Your Senses** Write the headings shown below on a sheet of paper. Then write the following sense words under the correct headings: wet, loud, blue, fresh, spicy, huge, soft, bitter, green, sweet, round, salty, square, hum, little, crash, red, smoky, stale, warm, rough. Some words will go under more than one heading.

Color	Size and Shape	Sound
Smell	Touch	Taste

Now add at least two words of your own under each heading.

Write each sentence below, using a sense word in the blank. Remember that a sense word tells how something looks, sounds, smells, tastes, or feels. Share your sentences with your class.

1. The hikers felt the spray from the ___ waterfall.
2. The ___ roses grew on the wooden fence.
3. Joseph heard the car's ___ brakes.
4. The horses pulled the wagon over the ___ road.
5. The engine ___ as the plane took off.
6. David touched the rabbit's ___ fur.
7. The air smelled ___ after the fire.
8. Anne made a funny face when she tasted the ___ lemon.
9. After the rain, the air smelled ___.
10. Jimmy tasted the ___ grapes.

- **Using Exact Words**   Rewrite each sentence below. Change the underlined word to a more exact word. Use the words in the box to help you.

1. Tall trees stood along the path.
2. Lisa ran to first base.
3. The bread smells good.
4. The colorful kites moved in the air.
5. A hurt puppy came to the door.
6. We followed a curved road up the mountain.

fresh
dashed
danced
elms
limped
winding

Rewrite the sentences below. Use exact words of your own to replace the underlined words.

1. The tourists went to Rome for a vacation.
2. Their vacation was very nice.
3. They saw many things in museums.
4. They enjoyed the good food.
5. Some of them walked to the top of a tower.

- **Proofreading**   Proofread these sentences. Each sentence has two mistakes. Write each sentence correctly. Use a dictionary if you need to.

1. jenny walked around the old bilding.
2. It was maid of gray stones
3. she sat in a pretty iron chare on the terrace.
4. In the garden she saw a beautifull Fountain.
5. birds splashed in the fountains cool water.

More Practice

- **Pronouns** Write the pronoun or pronouns in each sentence. Write *S* if the pronoun is singular. Write *P* if it is plural.

  1. Howard got into the car with Sue and me.
  2. I am sitting behind him.
  3. We are waiting for you.
  4. Can you help me with the groceries?
  5. I cannot lift them.
  6. They will fall unless you hold onto them.
  7. Are they too heavy for you?
  8. The snow fell on her.
  9. It made her very wet.

  Write a pronoun to replace the underlined words.

  10. Mother and I went to the library.
  11. The library is five blocks away.
  12. David was at the library.
  13. We saw two other friends there, too.
  14. Ms. Putnam is the librarian.
  15. Ms. Putnam found a book for mother and me.

- *I* and *me* Write the correct pronoun for each sentence. Write *subject* or *predicate* to tell where the pronoun is used.

  16. Jim and (I, me) went hiking.
  17. Dad gave Jim and (I, me) a map.

18. Jim and (I, me) walked all day.

19. Then it rained on Jim and (I, me).

- **Contractions**   Write a contraction for the two words.

  20. I am   **23.** they will   **26.** he is
  21. we will   **24.** I would   **27.** you are
  22. you have   **25.** I have   **28.** they have

- **Using Words Correctly**   Write the correct word to complete each sentence.

  29. We have (ate, eaten) breakfast.
  30. They (ate, eaten) breakfast two hours ago.
  31. Joe (gave, given) Pat a present for her birthday.
  32. He has (gave, given) her a book.

— Enrichment —

To play *Pronoun Baseball*, make a set of cards with a different pronoun on each one. Then make another set of cards with sentences like these. Leave a blank where a pronoun should go.

_____ hear the birds.
Come to the game with _____.

1. Choose two teams.

2. Each player gets a turn at bat. The batter draws one pronoun card and one sentence card. If the pronoun correctly completes the sentence, the player gets a hit. If it does not, it is a strike. Each batter plays until he or she gets a hit or strikes out (three strikes).

3. After one team gets three outs, the other team is up. Keep a record of the number of hits. The team with the most hits wins.

More Practice

- **Writing a Good Beginning**   A good beginning uses exact words. It makes readers want to keep on reading. Write a good beginning of one or two sentences for each story below.

    . . . José put the hurt bird in a warm box. He gave it food and water every day. Slowly the bird grew stronger. Sometimes it flapped its wings. One day José put the bird on the branch of a tree. The bird lifted its wings and flew away.

    . . . The old house was falling down on one side. Bats flew around the chimney. Jean and Mark walked softly up the porch steps. They stepped through the open door. A light flickered in the dark hall. The frightened children turned and ran. They didn't stop until they were all the way home.

- **Telling Enough**   Using enough details in your writing gives readers a clear picture of what happened. Rewrite each paragraph below. Add details so that the paragraph tells enough.

    One Saturday night Joe and I camped out at Boone River. We had a good time. The next day we went home.

    Our trip to Oregon was exciting. We took two weeks to drive across the country. On the way we met interesting people.

- **Writing a Good Title** A good title gives a hint about a story. It makes you want to read the story. Write a title for each story below. Remember to begin the first word and each important word with a capital letter.

The score was tied. Tim and Don were so excited! Which team would win? Then thick clouds darkened the sky. Raindrops started to fall, and the game was stopped. Tim and Don waited and waited. They hoped the rain would stop so the game could go on.

"Today is Dad's birthday," said Sue. "I don't have any money to buy a present. What should I do?"

"You don't need to buy anything," said Sue's mother. "Why don't you make something?"

"I don't have time," answered Sue. "I know what I'll do. I'll help Dad plant the vegetable garden. That will be a good present."

- **Proofreading** Proofread these sentences. Write each sentence correctly. There are two mistakes in each one. Look up words in a dictionary if you need to.

1. the Baxters went on a trip to the Grand Canyon in arizona.
2. How wide and depe the canyon was
3. Nellie tok pictures of the beautiful red Rocks.
4. The baxters rode mules to the bottom of the caynon.
5. inside the canyon they saw the Colorado river.

More Practice

- **Using a Dictionary** Write these words in alphabetical order.

airplane	around	aboard
agree	away	anyone
accident	adventure	asleep

- **Finding Words in a Dictionary** Here are three sets of guide words and a list of entry words. Write the guide words that you would find on the page with all of these entry words.

seize/sew	**sneeze/squawk**	**stamp/stone**
spring	sound	someone
snow	special	square

- **Choosing the Right Definition** Read the definitions of *season*. For each sentence below, write the number of the definition that goes with the word *season* in the sentence.

  sea·son (sē′ zən) **1.** One of the four parts of the year; spring, summer, autumn, or winter. **2.** A part of the year when something special happens: *football season; the rainy season.* **3.** To add extra flavor to food.

  1. I will <u>season</u> the soup with some pepper.
  2. Spring is my favorite <u>season</u> of the year.
  3. During harvest <u>season</u>, everyone on the farm helps out.

- **Using the Library**   Write each book title. Next to the title, write *fiction, nonfiction,* or *reference* to show the part of the library where you would find the book.

   4. *Science Experiments You Can Eat,* by Vicki Cobb, tells science experiments you can do with food.
   5. *Picture Atlas of the World* contains maps and facts about the world.
   6. *Little House in the Big Woods,* by Laura Ingalls Wilder, tells stories about an American pioneer family's life.

- **Using a Table of Contents and an Index**   Use the table of contents and the index to answer the questions that follow.

Contents		Index
1. Track and Field Games	4	baseball, 10–11, 24–25
2. Team Games	10	basketball, 12–13
3. Stick and Ball Games	23	bicycles, 65, 68, 70–73
4. Water Games	47	lacrosse, 19, 87
5. Games on Wheels	64	roller-skating, 74–76
6. Games of the World	82	running, 4–7
Index	111	swimming, 21, 47, 50–52

   7. What is this book about?
   8. How many chapters does this book have?
   9. What is the title of Chapter 6?
   10. On what page does the chapter on team games begin?
   11. On what pages can you read about roller-skating?
   12. Is ice-skating listed in this index?
   13. On what pages can you read about baseball?

More Practice

- **Telling Facts**   Write the number of each sentence below that tells facts.

  1. There are six states in New England.
  2. Red cars look better than blue cars.
  3. Six plus four equals ten.
  4. Apples taste better than peaches.
  5. Mrs. Ross is older than my father.
  6. Sleeping in a sleeping bag is fun.
  7. George Washington was the first president of the United States.

- **Keeping to the Main Idea**   The topic sentence tells the main idea of a paragraph. Read the paragraph below. Write the topic sentence. Think about the main idea given in the topic sentence. Then write the sentence that does not keep to the main idea.

  > Trees live for different lengths of time. Willow trees grow fast but do not live many years. Oak trees grow slowly and live for hundreds of years. The redwoods are America's tallest trees. A few giant sequoias are more than three thousand years old.

  Write the sentence in the paragraph below that does not keep to the main idea.

  > Some kinds of plants can grow only in water. Water lilies are rooted in the bottoms of streams, lakes, and ponds. Their blossoms float on top of the

water. The state flower of Iowa is the wild rose. Some water plants have no roots. They move around through the water.

- **Taking Notes**   Read each paragraph below. Write the topic sentence for each one. Take notes on the important facts in each paragraph.

    Some birds help to protect our trees. Woodpeckers make holes in trees for their nests. They eat insects in the trees. Nuthatches eat spiders' eggs, moths, and young beetles from tree trunks. Chickadees eat insect eggs from twigs and branches.

    Goldfish are very hardy. Even when they live in ponds, they don't freeze in winter. They can get used to hot or cold water. In the winter, goldfish almost go to sleep. They drop to the bottom of the pond and bury themselves in the soft mud until spring.

- **Proofreading**   Proofread each paragraph below. There are five mistakes in each one. Write the paragraphs correctly. Use a dictionary if you need to.

    The steam engine was developed by james Watt in 1760. The steam engin was the first machine that made power. the first steam engines pumped water out of mines. Later they was used to make boats and trains move

    the trap-door spider digs a hole, or burrow, in the ground. It covers the hole with a trap dor. The spider takes about sixteen hours to make the hole The spider hide in the burrow for protection. Sometimes it opens the door to katch an insect to eat.

More Practice

- **End Marks** Write each sentence. Use the correct end mark.

   1. Barry and Martha went to the museum
   2. Will they like the paintings
   3. What bright colors they saw
   4. How many paintings did they see
   5. They went home when they were tired

- **Commas in a Series** Write each sentence. Put commas in the correct places in each series.

   6. The spring months are March April May and June.
   7. Leaves fall in September October and November.
   8. Is spring summer fall or winter the best time?
   9. It is very hot in June July and August.
   10. It often snows in December January and February.
   11. September April June and November have thirty days.
   12. My friends' birthdays are in March August and October.
   13. There are holidays in October November and December.

- **Quotations** Write each sentence. Add quotation marks, commas, end marks, and capital letters.

   14. Mrs. Martin said today we will start making pottery
   15. Jeff asked how do you make pottery

16. Mrs. Martin asked have you ever played with clay
17. Ruth answered i made my mother a dish
18. Carla asked can I paint my pottery
19. Mrs. Martin said we will all paint the pottery
20. Jeff asked can I touch this piece
21. Mrs. Martin answered be careful
22. Jeff said i won't drop it
23. Mrs. Martin exclaimed it's time to be potters

● **Using Words Correctly**   Write the correct word to complete each sentence.

24. Father has (took, taken) the clothes to the laundromat.
25. He (took, taken) all the dirty clothes with him.
26. Father said, "(Bring, Brought) the soap."
27. Mary (bring, brought) the soap with her.

Enrichment

You have learned when to use three different kinds of end marks. You have also learned when to use commas in a series and quotation marks.

Now dream up some "personal punctuation." Invent three new kinds of punctuation marks and draw them on a sheet of paper. Beside each mark, tell how it is used. How does your new mark make the meaning of a sentence clear?

Now write five sentences using your new punctuation marks. Show how they are used.

More Practice

● **The Five Parts of a Letter**   There are five parts in a letter: the heading, the greeting, the body, the closing, and the signature. Look at each part below and write which part it is.

1. I'll meet your train at 6:30 Friday morning. Have a good trip!
2. Lucille
3. 406 Wood Street
   Springfield, Vermont 02167
   April 14, 1983
4. Dear Jordon,
5. Your sister,
6. The campgrounds are open from April until October. What month would you like to go camping? I would like to go in spring or fall. It's too hot in the summer.
7. Your friend,
8. Dear Meg,
9. Route 1, Box 121
   Rockfish, Maryland 18037
   December 1, 1983
10. Jonathan

   Choose a heading, greeting, body, closing, and signature from the list above. On a sheet of paper, write the parts in the correct form for a letter. Remember to indent paragraphs and to use correct punctuation.

- **Addressing an Envelope** An envelope needs two parts: an address and a return address. Write the name of the part that is missing from each envelope below.

1.

```
Wendy Fong
450 West Boulevard
Chicago, Illinois 60632
```

2.

```
John Heath
202 Pleasant Road
Atlanta, Georgia 30340
```

Draw an envelope on a sheet of paper. Address the envelope, using the address below. Use your own name and address in the return address.

Mr. Dale Santoro
85 Penwick Lane
Euclid, Ohio 44121

- **Proofreading** Proofread the addresses below. Write them correctly. The first address has three mistakes. The second one has four mistakes.

Ms. Clara banks
114 blossom Street
Charlottesville, virginia 22906

Mr. Sam Russo
24 Mountain Street
north conway New hampshire 03860

More Practice

- **Adjectives**   Write each sentence. Circle the adjectives. Underline the nouns they describe.

    1. The purple lilacs bloomed in the large yard.
    2. The white cat crept under the low bushes.
    3. Yellow flowers grew in the small garden.
    4. The gardener wore a green hat.
    5. He planted a small tree in a deep hole.
    6. He trimmed the tall hedges.
    7. White petals fell from a flowering tree.
    8. A gentle rain fell on the rolling lawns.

- **Using Adjectives**   Write an adjective to describe or tell how many for each underlined noun.

    9. The swimming pool was in the ____ park.
    10. There were ____ people in the pool.
    11. It was a ____ day.
    12. The ____ water felt good.
    13. My ____ friends went swimming with me.
    14. We brought ____ towels.

- **Using _a, an,_ and _the_ and Comparing with Adjectives**   Write each sentence. Use the correct word in ( ).

    15. (An, The) diamond is the (harder, hardest) stone.
    16. Is (a, an) diamond (prettier, prettiest) than (a, an) emerald?

17. My sister has (a, an) opal on (a, an) gold chain.
18. The diamond is one of (a, the) (brighter, brightest) stones.
19. Yesterday was (damper, dampest) than today.
20. Today is the (hotter, hottest) day of (an, the) week.
21. (A, The) nights are (cooler, coolest) than (a, the) days.

- **Using Words Correctly**   Write the correct word to complete each sentence.

22. Jane went (to, two, too) the pet shop.
23. She bought (to, two, too) fish.
24. She bought some food for them, (to, two, too).
25. She gave the fish (to, two, too) Kim.
26. (There, Their) were other fish in Kim's tank.
27. (There, Their) fins were bright red.

Enrichment

You will need two teams to play this guessing game. Each team should think of one person (*Guess Who*), one place (*Guess Where*), and one thing (*Guess What*). The team should also make a list of five adjectives to describe each of the three nouns.

Start with *Guess Who*. One team asks, "Who are we thinking of?" The team members take turns giving the adjectives as clues. After each clue, a player on the second team tries to guess the answer. If a player guesses correctly before all the clues have been given, the second team gets one point. If no one guesses correctly, the first team gets a point. After each team has played *Guess Who*, play *Guess Where* and *Guess What*. The team with the most points wins.

More Practice

- **Telling Things in Order** Below are the beginning and ending for two stories. Write the middle of each story. Tell the things that happened in order.

1. Beginning

Martha was so excited! She ate her breakfast as quickly as she could. Then she grabbed her sweater and dashed to the front door.

"Good-bye, Mom," Martha called, as she skipped down the porch steps.

It was Saturday. Uncle Bert had given Martha five dollars. She knew exactly what she would do with it.

Ending

Uncle Bert placed his hand on Martha's shoulder. He looked at her with a warm smile.

"I'm proud of you, Martha," he said. "You have made your grandmother very happy."

2. Beginning

Barbara and Jean were tired. They had been exploring the woods all afternoon. As the sun sank lower in the sky, they decided to go home.

They walked and walked, but every step took them deeper into the woods. They looked in every direction. The dark forest surrounded them. Where was the path that would take them home?

"We are lost," Jean said softly.

Ending

Barbara and Jean sat on the thick rug by the warm fireside. Their dog Scout settled down beside them. The girls were happy to be home.

- **Writing a Good Ending** Read the beginning and the middle for the story below. Then write two endings for the story. Tell which ending you like best, and why.

After that long, happy summer, Jeff went to the new school on Central Street. His sister, Nella, went away to school.

Jeff worked hard in school as Nella had told him to do. Jeff wrote letters to her. He waited and waited for an answer. Sometimes he would stop his work and wonder, "Will I ever see my sister again?"

- **Proofreading** Proofread these sentences. Write them correctly. Look up words in a dictionary if you need to. You should find nine mistakes in all.

1. I'll go to the store on tuesday.
2. That's the day mr. jones gets fresh bread
3. Fresh bread makes good sandwiches and tost.
4. don't you think fresh bred is good
5. i knew you would.

Proofread the paragraph below. Write the paragraph correctly. You should find thirteen mistakes.

i like to take walks with my dog. If he's feeling friskee, he runs ahead of me if it's too hot, he falls behind. he always stays nearby. he liks it best when we go to the creek then he can have a cool swim. He is always ready when i say, "Want to take a walk

INDEX

Numbers in **bold type** indicate pages where item is introduced.

Numbers in *italic* indicate further practice.

Credits

Cover and Title Page Photography by Olmsted Studio

Illustration

Jan Brett: pp. 104–105, 107–112, 194, 197–199, 201–204, 248–249.

Lorinda Bryan Cauley: pp. 246–247.

Laura Cornell: pp. 244–245.

Michael Deraney: pp. 132–134, 137, 139, 141–143, 254–256, 258, 262–263.

Joanna K. Fabris: pp. 11–17, 19, 21, 23–24, 44–49, 51, 53–55, 57, 59–61, 82–85, 87–89, 91, 93–94, 96–97, 99, 116–117, 119–120, 123–125, 180–181, 183, 185–189, 208–210, 213–214, 216–217.

David Kelley: pp. 113, 205.

Deborah Roberts Kirk: pp. 68, 71, 73, 75–79.

Giulio Maestro: pp. 242–243.

James Marshall: p. 260 from *What's the Matter with Carruthers?* by James Marshall copyright © by James Marshall. Reprinted by permission of Houghton Mifflin Company.

Stella Ormai: pp. 224–226, 228–229, 231, 233, 235, 237, 239.

Heidi Palmer: pp. 150–155, 158.

David Rose: pp. 162, 164–168, 171–172, 174–175, 177.

Jill Weber: pp. 32–34, 36–38, 40–41.

Pat Wong: pp. 250–251.

Handwriting by Chris Czernota, Mary Keefe, and Mark Mulhall.

Photography

Burk Uzzle/Magnum: p. 8; Bill Binzen: p. 28; Eric Crichton/Bruce Coleman: p. 31; Bryce Flynn/Picture Group: p. 42; Linda Moore/Rainbow: p. 66; Dr. E. R. Degginger: p. 70; Jay Lurie: p. 80; P. Nelson/After Image: p. 102; Dan McCoy/Rainbow: p. 114; Tom Leigh/Rainbow: p. 130; Jack Spratt/Picture Group: p. 148; Jacana Kerban/The Image Bank: p. 157; Jeff Foot: p. 160; Varin Visage/Jacana, The Image Bank: p. 163; B. Carrey/Picture Cube: p. 178; M. Markin/Bruce Coleman: p. 192; Bill Binzen: p. 206; Bill Binzen: p. 222; Werner Meinel/Taurus: p. 240; Marjorie Pickens: p. 252.